A Woman's Guide To Empowered And Enhanced
Sexual Experiences In The Evolution Of Life

SEX
AFTER...

KANISHA L. HALL, M.D.

Lightning Fast Book Publishing, LLC
P.O. Box 441328
Fort Washington, MD 20744

Stay Connected with KaNisha L. Hall, M.D. www.drkanishalhall.com

All rights reserved. No part of this book may be reproduced or transmitted in any form or by any means—electronic, mechanical, photocopying, recording, or otherwise—without written permission from the author, except for the inclusion of brief quotations in a review.

The author of this book shares information to aid the reader in developing self-love and finding redemption. The information provided is based on the personal philosophy and experience of the author. The intent is to offer general information that, when applied, will aid readers in facilitating personal growth. In the event that you use any of the information in this book, the author and publisher assume no responsibility for your actions.

The publisher, Lightning Fast Book Publishing, assumes no responsibility for any content presented in this book.

Copyright © 2017 by KaNisha L. Hall, M.D. All rights reserved.

ISBN-10: 0-9974925-5-4
ISBN-13: 978-0-9974925-5-2

CONTENTS

Preface 7
Chapter 1: ...Your First Time 11
Chapter 2: ...Education 21
Chapter 3: ...Work 28
Chapter 4: ...Commitment 38
Chapter 5: ...Children 47
Chapter 6: ...Betrayal 58
Chapter 7: ...Divorce 69
Chapter 8: ...Failure 77
Chapter 9: ...Menopause 84
Chapter 10: ...Cancer 92
Chapter 11: ...Drugs 99
Chapter 12: ...Salvation 105
Chapter 13: ...Death 114
Chapter 14: ...Empowerment 122
Acknowledgements 129
About the Author 131

DEDICATION

*Nora, without you there would be no book and no me.
Alfred, Andre &Ava Grace, you complete me.(AAA)*

PREFACE

I had both personal and professional motivations to put pen to paper and map this journey of empowerment. I worked hard to successfully complete my medical training and provide optimal care. So when I anecdotally noticed better outcomes, prognosis, and pain control in patients who reported continued sexually activity throughout their illness, my personal and professional curiosity peaked. I thoroughly enjoyed my studies in sexual health and sexuality counseling. I could not keep these wonderful resources to myself. Being surrounded by beautiful, strong women birthed a desire to enhance their abilities to master the art of self-fulfillment. My newfound understanding of the intersecting dynamics of biology and sexuality made me an advocate for comprehensive healthy living. Now my message is more holistic and inclusive of preventive medicine, allopathic medicine, nutrition, and sexual health. I want my loved ones and patients to eat healthy, stay active, seek medical advice and implement healthy sex practices.

My mother probably thinks I wrote this book to embarrass her. That theory has to be the furthest thing from the truth. I wrote this book after being inspired by her journey. After my dad passed away, I moved back to my hometown to be closer to my mother. Living in my childhood home that held way too many memories of my beloved father was not an option. I purchased a home in Shreveport, Louisiana for both my mother and I to start anew. We grieved together and grew together. I had the cherished opportunity to get to know my mother as more than my mom but my best girlfriend. Before long, I learned my dad was the only man in her sexual repertoire. As a teenager she had left her parents' home to build a home with my dad, as his wife and mother of two. No degree I have or will ever obtain can give me more pride than teaching my mother how to be an independent, single lady. We learned together about household budgets, healthy lifestyle changes, self-awareness, and self-defense. I will admit taking great pleasure in making my mom uncomfortable with the sex talk. I also relish the fact that many will know this former Sunday School teacher owns a vibrator. However, if those inconsequential tidbits of information are the only things you take away from reading this book, I have failed you. More importantly, you have failed yourself.

I painstakingly unearthed some of the most vulnerable moments of my life and my mother's life to empower women to take on the difficult task of self-discovery, self-care, and self-pleasure. I wrote this book with a desire to reveal the innate gifts every woman holds in her possession to command their sexual prowess. This piece of literature is my way of paying homage to womanhood and giving life to a movement that acknowledges women as sexual beings. I wanted women to know their inherent power to fulfill their sexual desires. Every chapter aims to address the many stations most women find themselves in over the course of a lifespan that may also present roadblocks to their sexual satisfaction. Nonetheless, hurdles are meant to becleared. Rules are made to be broken. Limits are present to be transgressed. Hopefully this book can serve as a woman's guide to empowered and enhanced sexual experiences in the evolution of life.

SEX AFTER...

CHAPTER 1: ...YOUR FIRST TIME

Let us begin with a moment of silence in remembrance of our first sexual experience. Let us lay to rest the disheartening memory we commonly share of fumbling through an amateur attempt to reach the proverbial promised land, an orgasm. Every professional has to start as a novice, so take solace in good company. You are not alone. Few people describe their first time as anything more than an uncomfortable and embarrassing rookie premiere. The disappointing uneasiness and even pain after your first sexual encounter may be a distant recollection or a recent travesty. The anticlimactic fall from grace is inevitable. Still, the short-lived event can be used to set the stage for your next debut as a liberated and empowered sexual being. Now is the time to embark on this journey for knowledge, power, and sexual fulfillment. Your next first time is going to be fantastic. I can proclaim your future success with confidence, because I plan to give you the tools to discover what really gives you pleasure. I am here to bolster your fundamental desire for gratification. I believe every individual is innately gifted with everything needed to be pleased and to please others. But first, I want to focus on just you. I want to dismantle the falsehood that you need a partner for sexual fulfillment. Now do not get me wrong, sharing a sexual experience with another person can be another level of pleasure and gratification. However, in order to endow you with ownership of your sexual prowess, I need you to take responsibility for your own sexual enjoyment.

Permission Always Comes First

Again, think back to your first time. I do hope permission was requested and granted before any engaging in physical contact. Sex should never happen without permission. So at this very moment, give permission. Give yourself permission to explore the opportunity to find pleasure. The act of giving permission sets the scene to explore the thought of being aroused, pleased, and fulfilled. This progression is an active process that requires you to lower your inhibitions and be open to receiving a sensual gratification.

Pleasure can be given from non-sexual activities. A professional massage is not sexual but your senses may be heightened to the pressure and touch. I have had a massage that literally ached so good that I was left in a breathless satiety. It is a normal response to receive pleasure from human touch. If you notice an inner heat, tingle, or any manifestation of pleasure due to your masseuse's touch, you owe it to yourself to try to recreate that sensation for yourself, by yourself. Give yourself permission to arouse yourself.

Orgasms are not Unicorns

Unicorns are mythical creatures of questionable existence. Likewise, some women believe orgasms are something people write and talk about but few actually confess to experiencing. Women want to know if orgasms are real, and the answer is yes.

Although only 1 in 3 women will report ever experiencing an orgasm, they are not mythical figments of imagination. Orgasms may be an endangered species, but they are not extinct. Physical touch, pressure, and caress have the ability to stimulate a chemical, hormonal, and emotional response in a woman's body. Muscle contractions, changes in body temperature, and the release of pleasure neurotransmitters have been witnessed and documented. I will not definitively say the ground will shake and the heavens will open for you. I can, however, say that you will feel something, anything. Women have described climaxing as a powerful heat, an exploding disembodiment, and overwhelming flood of pure pleasure. Orgasms are not passive, but a progression. First, you have to be aroused, stimulated. Repetitive stimulus intensifies into the sweet bliss of climax. This amplification is achieved with varying degrees of ease and difficulty. The intensity of climax also varied from individual to individual. You will never know where you fall on the spectrum until you embark on the quest to find out.

Before you commence any expedition, you have to define your current position in life and your desired destination. Almost every person reading this book will have a different station in life. Hopefully, we can all agree our destination is one of sexual health, pleasure, and fulfillment. An orgasm is a complex combination of emotional and physical climax brought on by an immensely pleasurable experience. Not everyone needs an explosive climax to feel sexually fulfilled. Essentially, pleasure is the single requirement. Furthermore, if you are one of the many women who seek the once-thought-to-be-elusive bliss of ecstasy, I can help you with your pursuit.

Envision Ecstasy

Before my first time, I imagined my first sexual experience would be akin to a romance novel or soap opera. Soft music would play and candles would adorn a silk-draped den of passion. I anticipated passionate kissing that would fade to a black abyss. Then the darkness would give way to bursting fireworks across a moonlit sky. Long gone are those disillusions of a hormone-intoxicated vixen. Now I know better. I know exactly how to describe the explicit, carnal delight I seek. I like to think of my orgasm as an exhilarating slide down an ice cream slope into a pool of warm chocolate. There is slipping, sliding, and shaking bordering on convulsions. All to be followed by a rush of energy as I then melt into a warm, sweet abyss. Before any of my fantastic illusions came to fruition, I had to imagine all I wanted it to be in my reality. I had to really allow myself to conceive these thoughts of debauchery. I want my reality to transcend the boundaries of the love scenes we often see in movies and on television. I want my life experiences to border on pornography. I refuse to believe that these thoughts make me dirty or flawed. These thoughts make me liberated and uninhibited. These thoughts help me achieve satiety of the sexual kind. Again, it started with envisioning my sugar-coated plummet into the depths of indulgence.

Your first exercise requires you to envision everything you believe an orgasm should entail. Allow yourself to possibly feel something so good your body aches for it. You have to bring these thoughts to your mind's eye and paint a picture. Then you have to transfer the picture to paper. Your next exercise requires you to write down everything you hope your ascent or descent to divine ecstasy will be. Be descriptive and precise. Write out in detail how you hope your body responds and the sensations you hope to feel in response to sexual stimulation. Realize if you cannot bring yourself to write about having an orgasm or simply feeling pleasure, you are more than likely not ready to truly experience any of these intense emotions. It is quite all right if you are not ready. But it is not acceptable to never be ready. Conjure up the thoughts, then the courage, to bring pen to paper and write down what you want. The thoughts should not live forever in your mind. Putting your imagery on paper makes it real. These thoughts on paper are the blueprint, your map. Prepare yourself to be overwhelmed. You need the ability to foresee your arrival at the point of climax in order to navigate your journey.

Pleasure Mapping

If I were to ask you how to get to your local grocery store, I am sure you could give me directions to its location with ease. You can give me these directions because I assume your local grocery store is a place you frequent. Now I ask, how do you expect a partner to blindly navigate your erotic zones and stumble upon the exact spot with the precise amount of pressure to send you on a rocket ship ride to the orgasmic bliss? These notions are the unrealistic expectations we must shatter. You have to know your body, know what feels good, and know what feels great.

Touch yourself. Most women view masturbation as a dirty act. We all assume every man we know masturbates, yet most women do not engage in regular self-pleasure. Masturbation is simply the act of pleasing yourself, and it should become a part of your regular routine of health practices.

Liberate your mind from the negative connotations that you may have previously associated with masturbation. Again, I remind you to give yourself permission to feel. Normalize the thought of bringing yourself pleasure with an everyday act like applying lotion. While in the act, take a moment to slow your breathing and motions of your hands to simply take notice of how your skin feels. Be aware of any changes in your breathing that may occur when you caress certain regions, such as earlobes, or the area behind your knees. When you lather soap on your body during a bath or shower, take a moment to notice how good it feels to apply varying levels of pressure to your neck, your arms, your breasts, and your thighs. Be thorough with your cleanliness and your exploration. You should know every area of your body that craves special attention. If I give you a blank diagram of the human body, you should be able to shade in every area of your body that cause some form of arousal. This exercise is called pleasure mapping. It is imperative that you are thorough and uncover all those hidden areas beyond the obvious genitals and breasts because your personal map is the answer key. Your map will have all the right answers for partner to attempt to get correct. No more and never again will the blind be leading the blind. You will be able to offer accurate directions to those erotic zones you map out. This exercise is another tool to help you reach your ultimate destination.

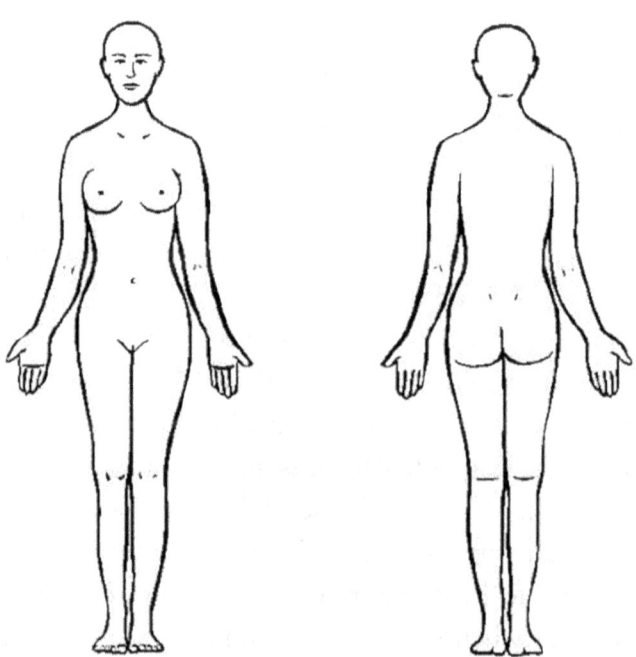

Pleasure Mapping:

1. Personalize the diagram to resemble you. Add hair, facial features, etc.
2. Explore your anatomy to identify specific areas that respond to stimulation.
3. Shade the diagram with colors to represent the areas that enjoy stimulation, pleasure points.
4. For couples, give your partner a blank diagram to shade based on areas they believe bring you pleasure.
5. Compare the diagrams.

My Sex, My Health

Beyond mapping your pleasure points, you should also be prepared to navigate the inner depths of your vagina. As a clinician, I am sincerely befuddled by so many women who regularly allow strangers to invasively probe their vagina during their annual visit to the Obstetrician/Gynecologist for the sake of preventative health and screening. At least once a year, a woman will go to the doctor and allow him or her to insert a foreign, hard and cold object into their most intimate space, and yet these same women will not touch their own vulva, clitoris or vagina for the sake of sexual health. Women will probe their own breasts in search of any possible deformity indicative of cancer. And again they will not massage their breasts and nipples to evoke pleasurable sensations or arousal. We have and will allow our partners to poke and prod the innermost depths of our vaginas in hopes they find that magical spot that curls our toes. I challenge you to plunge into the depths of your own sexual exploration. My hope is to plant the seed of desire in your cognition to take back ownership of your sex and sexuality. I want every reader to have a yearning for the knowledge of self. I want everyone to make it a priority to indulge in self-pleasure and gratification.

Sexual health and the benefits of regular sexual activity are all too often not a priority to women. I am telling you sex is good for your mind, body, heart, and soul. Sexual health is a part of being generally healthy. Sex must be a priority. We use our hands regularly to clean our bodies, moisturize our skin and sometimes massage achy muscles. We do these things because we believe our bodies need to cleaned, our skin needs to be nourished, and our touch has healing properties. All of these beliefs are very much true. I need you to also believe your body needs pleasure to be in good health. The benefits of sexual activity are far too numerous to list. Regular sexual activity has similar benefits of regular exercise on the human body. Sex improves cardiovascular and heart health while also lowering blood pressure. Sex increases your immunity to help prevent and fight disease. Sex reduces your risk for certain types of cancer. Sex reduces stress and improves sleep habits. Sex enhances your mood and helps fight depression. Furthermore, the more you have sex, the more you can naturally increase your libido and desire for that good feeling that comes along with it. Your body will crave the goodness. So give your body what it wants and needs.

My matriculation in medical school began with an intense study of all things normal. We studied normal anatomy and normal physiology. Our professors and instructors wanted every medical student to have a strong grasp on all the parts that are normally present and how each part normally works. A doctor cannot diagnose illness and disease before that doctor can identify what is normal. Likewise, you are categorically unable to recognize unhealthy behavior without a working knowledge of healthy sexual activity. The safest sexual practices begin with you. I am unaware of any sexually transmitted diseases conveyed via masturbation. Pleasing yourself also allows you to gage appropriate responses to stimulation. When you are aroused, your vagina should secrete a varying amount of fluid in response to being stimulated. This is a normal physiologic response. These secretions are present to naturally lubricate you vagina for intercourse and penetration. When you massage your clitoris, your vagina in turn should lubricate itself. If you are aware this is a normal response, you can also deduct that an abnormally dry vagina needs to be addressed. Also, you should know how the act of massaging your erotic zones again aids in lubricating your vagina during intercourse. Waiting until a penis is knocking at the door to your vaginal vault is not the time to discover your inability to self-lubricate. I want you to be confident everything is in good working order. Test drive your high-powered, throttling love making machine before you let anyone else get behind the wheel. In addition, if you can easily navigate your own body to climax, imagine how you can direct a partner to your desired destination.

Master Masturbation

Repetition is key. I fully expect you to fumble through your first few attempts to navigate your erotic zones. Hopefully just like rookies graduate to the major leagues, your novice experimentation propels you to mastering the art of masturbation. Yes, self-pleasure is truly an art form. Sex is a form of communication that requires a unique skill set. You have to find your love language. You need to know how your body likes to communicate and the manner in which your body like to be spoken to in order to be stimulated. Do you prefer a soft gentle touch? Would you like a firmer deep caress? I challenge you to try different temperatures. Rub an ice cube over some previously discovered pressure points. In turn, try massaging your muscles with a warm towel. It has already proven that the most efficient way to learn a new language is to immerse yourself in the culture and repetition. Your sexual immersion begins seduction. Treat yourself. Become the expert in all things you. I cannot tell you exactly what you like. I can only give you guidance and the tools to figure it out. Reference your pleasure map. By all means when you stumble upon anything that feels good, do not stop. When you discover a new erotic zone, plant your flag and own it. Own your body. Rediscover your sexual self every time you engage in self-pleasure.

The Next First Time

These are new experiences, and you must also give yourself permission to fail. Nothing worth having in my life has ever come easy. You cannot give up and resign yourself to a life without sexual pleasure. A life devoid of pleasure defines misery. I could never accept that fate, and I hope you will join me in my journey to promote sexual awareness, health and fulfillment. I want you to know that no one is born inherently good at sex. Sex is art, and pleasure requires practice. Keep practicing until you have unlearned every clumsy and awkward behavior of the first time. Be a professional at navigating yourself to pleasure. Every step toward self-gratification brings you closer to your destination of fulfillment. I have a feeling after your first self-induced orgasm, you will find your way back to that sweet ecstasy time and time again.

SEX AFTER…

CHAPTER 2: …EDUCATION

Whether you graduated with honors from an Ivy League institution of higher learning or you barely skated through the school of hard knocks, I find so many are still oblivious and ignorant to the basics of sexual education. Before we proceed on our quest for sexual empowerment, I feel everyone could use a basic refresher in human anatomy. Many women incorrectly refer to the visible lips of their sex organs as their vagina. In fact your externally visible organs, the labia majora and minora, actually make up your *vulva*. Your vagina is the inner passage-way that ends at your cervix. Your cervix is in turn located at the opening of your uterus, better known as the womb. It is empowering to know that life is held in the sex of a woman. This precious gift is to be honored and respected.

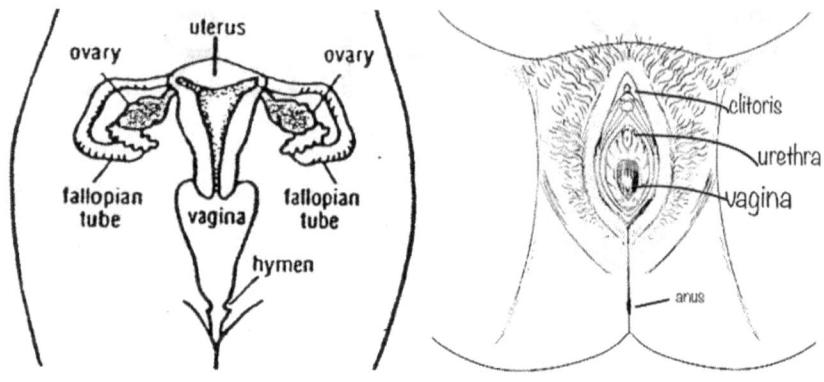

Also, it is of great benefit to know the location of your sex organs in relation to neighboring organs such as the bladder and intestines. Your bladder is a part of your urinary tract. Your intestines and colon are a part of your gastrointestinal tract. Both of these systems remove waste from your body every day. If for any reason you sense any irregularity in these organs, I am sure you will not hesitate to seek out why and how to fix the problem. Most people will agree that the proper function of our bladder and colon are essential to good health. Beyond reproduction and holding the seeds of life, your sex organs are also key to other important aspects of your health such as hormone production. Hormones are the chemical messengers of the body with numerous functions including regulating temperature, emotions and moods. We as women from early pubescence await the commencement of our menstrual cycle. We plan our lives around our menses.Needless to say, your sex organs are important. Therefore, I want you to be equally as concerned and committed to maintaining sexual health. I also want you to come to the realization that our wombs are not to be revered only as vessels of reproduction. Every individual is more than flesh and bone. We are a complex makeup of body and soul. As physical is to spirit, biology is to sexuality.

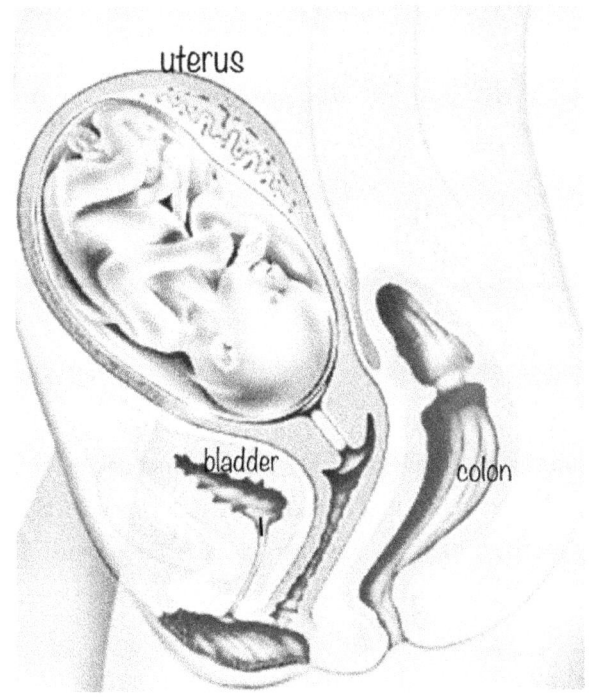

Cross-section of uterus, bladder, intestine.

Biology vs. Sexuality

Your anatomy is a part of your biology, which is determined by your genetic makeup. Your biology is genetically predetermined by chromosomes and genes. If you have two X chromosomes, you are genetically identified as female. If you have one X and one Y chromosome, you are genetically identified as male. These chromosomes contain scores of genetic coding for what sexual organs you possess. Males and females have distinctly different sex organs and hormone profiles. Your biology and sexuality are intertwined. Your sexuality maybe influenced, but not necessarily predetermined, by your biology.

Table 2:1 Sexual Blueprint

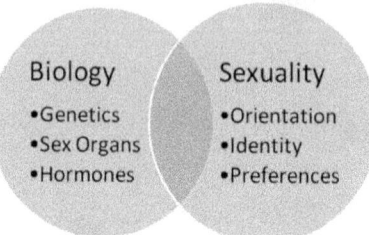

Your sexual blueprint is a manifestation of both biology and sexuality. Sexuality is a summation of several principles, such as your sexual orientation, identity, and preferences. Your sexuality and how you identify yourself is a piece of your complex individuality than is not always so cut-and-dried. I prefer to think of sexuality as a fluid entity. By fluid, I mean ever changing, evolving, and hopefully progressing.

As a clinician, I do not assume the sexual blueprint of my patients based on their biology or genetic makeup. I feel each individual has to define their sexuality. No one should be labelled lesbian, gay, bisexual, transgender, or queer. A person has every right and liberty to identify as heterosexual, lesbian, gay, bisexual, transgender or queer. I do not mean queer in a derogatory context, but non-vanilla. Sexual orientation, identity, and preference are personal liberties not to be taken for granted or dismissed. Society continues to debate what determines these parts of our individuality. We may never fully understand each individual's multifaceted blueprint, but respect, acceptance, and love are essential.

Health Class May Have Failed You

There is not a lot that I remember from health class in grade school. However, I do remember the most grotesque pictures of disease-ridden genitals. I believe these tactics were used to deter sex in that adolescent population. Conversely, the thought that someone would risk such a horrific fate peaked my curiosity. Even at that young age, I wondered what could be worth the risk of deformity or much worse death. At that time, sex had no value to me, but even in my youth I had grasped that fact that my safety and life were priceless. Unlike your grade school health class, I presently promote sexual activity, as long as it's safe sex. Your vagina is a unique, magical flower to be safeguarded and revered. Safe sex is the only sex worth practicing. With that being said, I still wonder why anyone would risk their safety and health.

Sexually transmitted diseases and infections are caused by bacteria, parasites, and viruses. These infections are dangerous and possibly fatal. Human Papilloma Virus (HPV) is a sexually transmitted virus linked to cervical cancer. HIV/AIDS can cause long-term disability with complications that may lead to death. Sexually transmitted infections are prevented by safe sex practices, such as using condoms and other barriers during sexual activity. While it's true I want to embolden your inner sexual prowess, I also want all readers to be conscious of their safety and health. No sex is worth your life.

See One, Do One, Teach One

Medical school holds so many fond memories for me. My quest for sexual empowerment commenced on the campus of Howard University in the College of Medicine. My instructors would often employ a "see one, do one, teach one" philosophy for learning new concepts, practices and procedures. I still use this method of teaching to this day with my students. First, you observe a technique. Then you must actually repeat the process you observed first-hand. Lastly, your ability to impart knowledge and skill of what you have seen and done further demonstrates an ascertained level of proficiency. One might wonder how these principles can be applied to sex. Well, I suggest you watch porn, masturbate, and teach your partner how you need to be pleased. See porn. Do you. Teach him or her.

School is Always in Session

Respect the journey. An entire life spent learning is definitely not time wasted. On one hand, I do believe we are born with innate abilities to navigate the basics of life and accomplish goals. On the other hand, I also believe life, time, and circumstances teach and lend us tools to progress on our journey. Some lessons seem to require trial and error. I try not to say I don't like something until I have tried it at least once. Being open to different sexual experiences and activities does not make me a hedonist creature, but an open individual who lacks inhibition. If a person has the desire and means to travel the world and experience different cultures, society is not quick to brand that individual a vagabond, vagrant, or tramp. More than likely, that person will be admired and thought of as well travelled. Upon their return, one might seek them out to hear about their adventures and inquire about all the things they may have learned. Similarly, sexuality is its own unique expedition. Sex is not nasty or dirty. Every life is a product of sex. Sexuality is a fluid river that feeds life. Where you start your voyage for sexual fulfillment is not where you finish. As an adult, I look similar to my infant self but definitely not identical. Likewise, my sexual blueprint in my twenties is not identical to that of my thirties. I very well may regress, digress, or progress. I am not sure exactly what my sexual blueprint will look like in my forties. I just know I never want to be stagnant.

Every sexual being has a journey riddled with lessons learned and hopefully more lessons to be learned. I never want to stop learning. I gladly confess I do not know everything there is to know about sex. Likewise, I am also happy to proclaim my eagerness to learn. I am dedicated to expanding my knowledge through reading, dialogue and especially hands-on interactive experiences. I am committed to my sexual education. I am devoted to the mastery of my own pleasure and fulfillment. You should be as well.

SEX AFTER...

CHAPTER 3: ...WORK

Anxiety and hesitancy are normal responses to new challenges. I can remember graduating from every level of higher education with butterflies in my belly. Humans naturally fear the unknown. What is coming next? You have to be confident that whatever learning processes you have gone through did indeed teach you something. Honestly, I believe life is the best classroom to lend you the tools necessary to tackle the vast unknown. Fear not and know you have what you need to get what you want. Your first day on any job is a test of fortitude. You may not know anyone or where anything is located. However, you should know your purpose and what you are on the premises to accomplish.

Usually, your employer will give you a job description either before or during the application process. This description should reveal any prerequisites and the tasks expected for the person who holds the position. To avoid any embarrassment, it would behoove you to gage if you are indeed qualified to apply and carry out the duties of a job. These considerations should take place prior to interviewing to avoid wasting anyone's time. To ascertain your readiness to embark on any career will require a thorough self-assessment. What are your skills, assets and availability? Also, what do you hope to gain from the employment?

Just as past experiences have taught us lessons to advance our careers, we have some lessons to unlearn. Disassembling years, possibly decades, of falsehoods disguised as social norms can be overwhelming. As little girls, most women are indoctrinated with notions of chasteness. Maybe you were told that women are to be seen and not heard. I am here to liberate you from these longstanding strongholds. In this new age of women spearheading corporations, leading healthcare initiatives and running for president, surely you can find the courage to explore and unleash your once depressed sexual prowess. So let's get to work.

Building Your Resume

Think back to your days as a young adult when one of your main goals was to start a career. Some go to college, trade school, or enter into the workforce with hopes of being promoted up the ranks. No matter what path taken, at some point you will have to go through the application process. An essential piece of that application is your resume. A resume is a listing of your educational experiences, synopsis of any previous positions held, and may also include some other accomplishments or certifications. Listing your training and work history allows you and your future employer to determine if you are a favorable candidate for a particular vacancy or appointment. Productive corporations do not employ any and every person applying, just like I do not want just any warm body sharing my bed. We all want qualified individuals.

Now, let's discuss the necessary components of your sexual resume. Your sexual resume is by no means a list of sexual conquests or partners. This resume is a notation of acquired skill sets that depict your willingness and ability to accept and offer pleasure. Sex is a form of communication, or conversation. The exchange implies both giving and receiving. An above average candidate must be able to explicitly express their wants and desires, as well as receive instructions and reciprocate.

I am well versed in my abilities of sexual exchange because I am receptive to the pleasure I give myself. Mastering the art of masturbation is key to self-assurance, bordering on arrogance, that you can also seduce and bring another person to the brink of carnal bliss. Similar to my first day on any job, I had to locate the things I needed to get the job done. I have fumbled through exploring my anatomy. In the beginning I knew exactly where my clitoris was located, I just was not quite sure what I should do with my pleasure mound. Nevertheless, immediately after my finger touched my hooded G spot, a shock wave shot up my pelvis and spine. It seemed as if I had found my sexual power switch. At some point in your life, I hope you give yourself permission and take the plunge. I can admit that getting started is usually the hardest part. Then you can advance beyond those amateur attempts to stimulate and arouse yourself for pleasure. Repeating the seductive process over and over fosters a level of comfort and ease. Hopefully, you will have a breakthrough and abandon inhibition to sexual whim. Be whimsical.

Your mouth is an ideal example of give and take. Your mouth is a composite of lips, teeth, gums, tongue, muscles, hard and soft palates. All of those parts have to work together, like complicated choreography, to accomplish important tasks. Your mouth receives food for nutrition. The complexity of mastication involves various muscle contractions. Your tongue houses millions of buds for tasting. In addition to taking in food, these same lips, tongue, and teeth convey our verbal expressions. We use our mouths to speak words, voice our emotions, and even give instructions.

Beyond conversing and consuming, your mouth is a valuable tool for giving and receiving pleasure. Oral sex is an attractive addition to any sexual resume. Now, I would be terribly amiss if I did not at least mention all the things your mouth can do. Again, I remind you to keep an open mind. I have been pleasantly surprised to speak with quite a few women who express curiosity about fellatio. The majority of these women just want to know how to get started. Fortunately, it is really simple. I don't mean to be crass, but a good head game is not Neurosurgery. If you can kiss lips, you can kiss genitals. It's all about communication. Start with your level of comfort, butterfly kisses. Advance at your own speed. Your mouth has that tongue for licking. If you are worried about the level of pressure and sucking, start on your partners fingers to judge how intense your sucking motions should progress. Then, you can feel a little more at ease with engaging their sexual organs.

Women have asked me how long they should be expected to give oral pleasure. That question tends to arise when you think of giving pleasure as a chore. In turn I ask, how long should you enjoy your dessert? I do not know about you, but I usually eat any sweet decadence until it is all gone. Honestly, giving pleasure with your mouth should be empowering. My competitive nature drives me do just about anything to make my partner squirm with pleasure. That's right. This is my turn to curl some toes. It makes me feel emboldened to cause the slow unnerving of another person with the sweep of my tongue. I actually get aroused at the sound of those reluctant guttural moans coming from a pleased recipient of my pleasure. And I am not stopping until I finish what I set out to accomplish. I want complete submission and compliance, like a boss. This level of confidence is birthed from my ability to please myself. I know it sounds selfish, but there is a reason my initial focus is always advocating exploration of your own erotic zones.

If You Want, You Better Work

Starting and building a career is by no means easy. The reasons why we are compelled to put forth the effort is commonly because we actually get something out of it. We all have wants and needs. We need food and shelter. We want the candy apple red convertible and travel to exotic lands. Both the necessities and the luxuries cost money. Thus, we rise and shine every morning in pursuit of financial gains that afford us our wants and needs. My grandmother taught me this very important lesson early in life: If you want, you better work. Just the same, if you want that hair-raising, nail-biting, toe-curling sex life, you had better be willing to put in some work. Hard work always pays off. Nonetheless, you cannot get to work until you first get the job.

Imagine the consequences of showing up for an interview with a polished resume but outfitted in disheveled attire. Would you trust a man that looks homeless to sell you a house? In order for others to have faith in your success, they must first believe. Even if they do not definitely know, they need to be able to trust your ability to accomplish the tasks at hand. Qualifications make a person look good on paper. A well-groomed applicant gives the impression that he or she possesses the physical aptitude do the job. I do not promote vanity. I do, however, advocate for good health. This concept encompasses physical, mental, and sexual health. I believe when you feel good on the inside, it manifests in your outer appearance. Preserve your physical health with regular visits to your physician, exercise, and eat healthy. Maintain your mental health by seeking counsel when needed, stress avoidance and stress relief. Sustain your sexual health with regular sexual activity, including masturbation, and good hygiene. Do not show up for a date with disheveled vulvas. Well-groomed genitals are visually enticing. Enticement incites arousal. Arousal begets stimulation, amplified to climax. And just think how it all started with a look. Always make your first impression your best impression.

I try my best to show up to work every day with a fresh perspective and a positive attitude. I am a consummate perfectionist. I push myself to be the best mother, physician, activist, and counselor I can possibly be for my daughter and our community. A new day is another opportunity to improve. Just as every new sexual encounter is a chance to better arouse, stimulate and climax. I owe it to myself to be a world-renowned expert in pleasing me.

Work Hard, Play Hard!

You looked the part and thus you got the part. Now what? Well, congratulations are in order. Gainful employment should not be taken for granted. Your daily grind affords you financial security for not just you, but also your family. It is important to enjoy the fruits of your labor, because life has a way of throwing unforeseen curve balls. At some point you will face obstacles and opposition in your career. Things do not always go as planned. Deadlines, holidays, illness, and many other stressors can slow your progress in general. Just know that slowing is not the same as ceasing to progress. I do not want you to ever think stopping is an option. Every chapter in this book is about the various circumstances we find ourselves in as women. These obstacles are opportunities to make adjustments to the normal routine. You have to shake things up every now and then. Track and field athletes jump and sprint in between hurdles. On this track that we call life, I want you to find your rhythm to jump your hurdles and keep sprinting.

Every day you may not be in the right state of mind or space to think about work, play, or sex. When I am truly grinding with work, I am consumed with the task at hand. After a full day of counseling, speaking, and writing about sex, I tend to find myself drained. Many times my physical and sexual health are neglected. My eating habits become unhealthy. I then, in turn, feel sluggish and unattractive. Furthermore, I lose any desire to please myself or anyone else. These moments have taught me to take regular inventory of my life. I realize a career, family, friendships, and other interests present separate demands on my time. All of these demands can collectively appear overwhelming. You will either find a way to juggle it all or let it fall apart. Before it gets to be unmanageable, organize and prioritize.

Time management is important to manage your career, family, friends and extracurricular activities. Arranging sexual activity requires some creativity, especially if you do not want to lose your spontaneity. Remember, sex should not only occur at night. Consider waking up a half hour early to make time for some self-gratification. I think it is an excellent way to start the day. You can also schedule a meal-time interlude at breakfast, lunch, or dinner. I would love for the world to see sex as a necessity, just like food. Maybe time does not permit sexual activity three times a day, but I challenge you to commit to at least three times a week.

We all put in the time and effort for the things that we really want. When you want a promotion on your job, you may find yourself working overtime and putting in more effort. You want your boss to take notice and think of you as an asset. I want you to think of sex as beneficial. I want you to take notice of how your mood and quality of life improves with regular sexual activity. I believe when you make sexual health and wellbeing a priority, you will find the time to feed your desire.

It Might be Time for a Career Change

When you lose passion for what you do, it may be time for a career change. I do not want to go to work every day, but most days I do love what I do. I say most days because everybody is allowed to dislike their job when it takes you away from something else you love. Sometimes, it pains me to leave my family and commit to those long days in the hospital, but then I see my patients. I quickly realize these patients need my care and also have family members that need them to be in good health. So I put my heart, mind, and soul into every case.

When you can no longer remember why you do what you do, it may be time for a career change. Yes we go to work to earn a living, but we should also receive some sense of fulfillment in return. Our careers should fulfill a sense of purpose in our lives. Every time I read emails from the ladies that attend my seminars for unveiling and empowering their sexual self, it motivates me to keep the conversation going. I promote sexual health because I personally know the benefits. As long as I keep enjoying sex, I will keep having sex. I will keep talking and writing about sex to any woman willing to receive the message.

When you do not see opportunity for advancement, I challenge you to make a move. Life is a progression. It has been wisely said, *if you are not moving forward, you are being left behind.* You may not need to change careers, but you may have to change something. We as women are all too familiar with glass ceilings, but glass is made to be shattered. Rules are made to be broken.

Playing it safe can be very boring. I do not want to work a boring job, live a boring life, or ever have boring sex.

Seeing is Believing

Successful people share a certain set of traits. They are competitive, goal oriented and hard working. Leaders are not resistant to change, but they adjust and adapt as needed. Accomplished people continue to be prosperous when they do not allow themselves to become satisfied with past endeavors and accolades. They continue to seek out the next challenge. Similarly, intelligent people do not know everything, but they do know when to ask for help.

So many times before I take on a "do-it-yourself" project, I will search the Internet for tutorial videos. Even after I have read the directions, I seem to be more successful after I can see another person complete the task. I am also encouraged when I can see the finished product. Similarly, pornography should be used as a research tool. Everyone is watching porn, so why aren't you? Pornography is not only for curious, hormone-driven teenage boys. Pornography is for all individuals and couples looking for entertainment or inspiration.

No matter what challenge you encounter in your quest for sexual empowerment, I am convinced there is a genre of pornography to inspire a solution. Unrelated to sexual orientation, I encounter more women who prefer lesbian porn. I have been told that they find naked women more aesthetically appealing. The more feminine appearance and likeness may make that type of porn more relatable. Again, I stress, enjoying same sex porn does not make anyone inherently gay. Any human being, no matter what sex or orientation, should be able to appreciate the beauty of the female body. Another popular genre of pornography has many websites dedicated to the sexual escapades of pregnant women. Some men are turned on by pregnant women, and pregnant women have surges of hormone that increases their appetite for intercourse. So when pregnant women are uncomfortable with the girth of their growing wombs and having trouble imagining how intimacy is even possible, I encourage them to watch porn.

I want you to have the tools of success. I challenge you to use porn to improve your sexual resume, resolve issues that may arise, and visualize the many possibilities. Push your imagination beyond its limits. Set your sights on those unbelievably gratifying sexual experiences. Then map your way to success. Seeing is truly believing. I believe you can succeed well beyond your wildest dreams, because I have seen it all done before. I am not just talking about pornography, but I am referencing my own life. I didn't wake up one day, put on a pair of leather chaps, and claim to be the dominatrix of desire. Well I may have dreamed about that once, and I very well may buy that Halloween costume. Presently, I am a summation of many trials and errors. I have failed until I found success, and I am still a work in progress.

SEX AFTER...

CHAPTER 4: ...COMMITMENT

Once you build your sexual resume and put on your business attire, you are ready to seek employment. I have been employed by companies, and I have owned my own company. I have navigated the advantages and disadvantages of both scenarios, and I know the importance of negotiating the terms of a contract in your favor. All is not fair in love and business, but almost everything is negotiable. In business the party with the most value and bringing the most worth to the deal usually does the least compromise. Thus, I find that I rarely have to compromise when the other party knows my dedication. Also, I never commit until I am confident I can provide all the required services in the agreement. I also will not sign a contract until I am satisfied that I am going to be adequately compensated for my service. I set the terms of my employment based on what is most beneficial to me and my family at the time. I know my worth. Some contracts are not worth signing. Some contracts appear too good to be true.

Relationships are no different. You have to carefully decipher what scenario works best for you. When you know your worth, you can seek an equally qualified party to engage. Compatibility is important, because a certain level of comfort is a prerequisite to share such an intimate exchange. When you are adequately coupled, you will be equivocally reciprocated. Identical does not necessarily mean compatible. I am not just talking about two people who enjoy doing the same things. I am talking two people with comparable desires to please and be pleased. If I am willing to put in the work, I want the same in return. I must have a partner that matches my hustle from the boardroom to the bedroom.

I do not discount that relationships are not for everyone, but I do believe *commitment* is indeed for everybody. You may be committed to the single life, and the principles of this chapter still apply to you. At times, I honestly think it takes just as much work, or maybe more, to remain single than being entangled in relationships. I should hope that if you are committed to yourself alone, you share that declaration with your romantic encounters. No one wants to be misled or allow someone to toy with their emotions. In return, I also hope your affirmations are respected. With that being said, I admire the devout singles. Furthermore, I challenge you to loyally preserve your identity and sexuality. Defy the odds, combat stagnant behaviors, and be innovative. It is your responsibility to nurture your sexual being and encourage your own growth. Conversely, polyamorous individuals are lovers of more than one partner. These relationships present another unique group that still require some level of commitment. When several people agree to be involved, each person must commit the collective betterment of the group as well as each individual involved. Whether you are committed to one or many, be true and faithful to yourself first. Be honest with yourself and take care to protect your emotional wellbeing.

Define Commitment

The insane have been committed to asylums because they are found to be a danger to themselves and/or others. In the same way, committing to the unknown is very dangerous practice. Commitment means different things to different people. Similar to sexual identity, I believe every individual should have their own definition and their own terms. You should know what you are willing to give and have realistic expectations of what you hope to receive as reciprocity. You can only make demands when you are very clear about what you want. It is your responsibility to know what you need in order to be content and never make assumptions.

Many women falsely presume commitment means monogamy. If you require monogamy, take nothing for granted and make it known. All parties have to agree on what defines unfaithfulness. I believe infidelity is any behavior that dishonors the commitment. Any communication, kissing, or intercourse that would lead another person to believe that they have a romantic involvement with my partner will be classified as betrayal. Conversely, I know quite a few people that disagree with my definition of cheating. Most will agree once genitals touch, then the lines of fidelity have been transgressed. The problem comes with the grey area. The communication that I find to be inappropriate, others may describe as innocent flirting. This example is one of many instances where disappointment can arise when you are not clear about what you want. Commitment represents a mutual understanding between all the parties involved. The terms need to be clearly defined to avoid misunderstanding and hurt feelings.

Set the Rules

Relationships are unique entanglements that work best with structure and boundaries. A sturdy foundation begins with honesty. Respect and trust are non-negotiable requirements. You have to respect yourself and follow your moral compass. I advise against entering into any agreement with people you do not respect. How can you trust a person you do not regard with integrity? Their word will mean nothing, making the commitment null and void. Someone you respect has value in your life, and their opinion matters. Someone you can trust is also someone who has your best interests in mind.

Safety should be a priority. All of these precautions build structure into the relationship for your protection, because you are ultimately responsible to ensure your emotional and physical welfare. Yes you should have a partner you can trust, but the only person's actions you can truly control are your own. I trust and know all humans to be flawed, including yours truly. So I tend to go the extra mile to safeguard my personal interests. I am unable to enjoy intimacy and pleasure at the expense of endangering my health and peace of mind. For me, safe sex is also non-negotiable. I know my HIV status and require my partner to do the same. I implore you to set your own standards to safeguard your emotional and physical wellbeing.

I feel all deal breakers should be addressed sooner rather than later. A true deal breaker is more than a preference of attraction. If you have firm opposition to a person who smokes, once you smell tobacco, do not waste precious time. Just walk away. Do not assume you will change a person or that the person will change for you. Believe their actions and verify their words. If you refuse to tolerate liars, quit giving Lying Larry chance after chance to prove to you he earned his nickname fair and square.

You should realize there is a difference between inspiring a person to be better and hoping a person will change. People are most definitely capable of bettering themselves and changing. True change, however, rarely comes at the request of another person. An individual has to have a desire to alter their behavior to initiate a true transformation. Never relinquish you right to choose, and always choose *you* first.

Wise counsel believes you should never go to the grocery store hungry. Hunger affects your cognition and rationality. A starving shopper will buy anything and everything in hopes of satisfying their appetite. In that moment, needs are neglected to appease overwhelming desire. Do not mistake your hunger for passion, or lust for love. Hunger and lust are often burdens of desperation. Passion is feverous desire. Love is unconditional admiration. Once hunger is foolishly satisfied you can still be left feeling empty and with regret. Passion is insatiable and requires repeated fulfillment. Have you ever had subpar to mediocre sex with someone you found physically attractive only because you were in a sexual drought? Did you regret it? I advise you to be wary of unions formed out of desperation. A woman who has mastered self-pleasure is unlikely to be desperate. She is a sexually fulfilled embodiment of confidence who is assured of her self-worth. Because of my masterful skill in self-gratification, I want more and feel I deserve more than a quick fix. I want the partner that came to impress me with his sexual resume. I want a mate that will acknowledge my standards to afford me the security I need. Then in that protected space, I am liberated to share my most inhibited and carnal thoughts. Then and only then will there be seduction, exploration, role-playing, and sensual acrobatics.

True commitment takes time. I will not argue for or against the validity of love at first sight. I just believe serious admiration and dedication are not acquired instantaneously. I am not one to haphazardly trust anyone or anything. I do my due diligence. My heart is too precious to throw caution to the wind. Knowing my value makes me hesitant to just give all this goodness away. Thus, I advise you not to rush. Give yourself time to assess what you want. Give a prospective partner time to reveal their true identity and earn your confidence. You need to truly assess if another person is deserving of all you can offer. Insecurity and doubt make for a very brittle foundation that easily crumbles intoregret and displeasure. You should desire a partner that fosters confidence and self-assurance. A good companion accepts that you are a flawed individual but also propels you to be a better person.

Break the Rules

Structured relationships are not where spontaneity and passion go to die. Commitment can be fertile soil for your flower of sexuality. When the foundation is laid in earnest with trust and security, a space is created where you can feel comfortable bearing your imperfections. Acceptance builds confidence. Confidence empowers expression to make your intimate requests known. This charged environment can birth the most mind blowing and sexually fulfilling connection. The goal should always be to build a sanctuary to explore your wildest dreams. You deserve a safe place to nakedly bare your deepest desires.

Because I trust myself implicitly, I feel comfortable exploring and navigating my own body for pleasure during masturbation. I also have not forgotten the work I put in to get this level of proficiency with pleasing myself. Adding a partner to the mix changes thecircumstances. This new situation requires a few adjustments to reestablish a certain level of comfort and stability.

Learn your partner. I think pleasure mapping is a great place to start. The more safe and secure you feel, the easier it should become to let loose and get a little crazy. Enjoy getting to know each other. Share your desires to try something new. Watch porn for inspiration. Do not allow your relationship to become stale or boring, but keep it liberating and stimulating.

Again, I know all of my dirty fantasies and most erotic aspirations. I am not willing to share these jewels with just anybody. Beyond my private pleasure sessions, certain things I choose to only disclose in the confines of the ultimate commitment of marriage. I believe nothing is off limits when you make a vow to love, honor and protect your partner for life. These personal beliefs are self-enforced rules of engagement that I established to protect myself. Rules are made to be broken, and I have made exceptions. Still, I have my guidelines in place to make decisions on my own terms and preserve my sanity and welfare.

Keep it Fresh

Whatever concessions you make to initiate a relationship should be sacrifices and behavior you can continue. Just the same, all that effort and energy you put into finding a mate will be needed to keep your mate. Maintaining a committed relationship requires hard work, time management, and exceptional communication skills. If you are a devout single you still have to put in the time and effort to ensure your self-care. Regular self-assessment of physical, mental, and sexual states allows you to evaluate your comprehensive wellness. Change happens without fail. So as individuals and circumstances evolve, any differences need to be communicated and addressed. Adjustments may benecessary.

Date purposefully. Dating is not reserved for singles and new couples in the early interviewing process. Dating allows you to reintroduce yourself to your partner as you both change over the course of time. Plan a few dates to keep the lines of communication open as life's hassles are indiscriminate to relationship status. Also, every now and again throw caution to the wind and keep it spontaneous. Make each moment count. You want to add pleasure and bliss to the life of your partner while they in turn do the same for you. Never take your partner or the relationship for granted. We all have choices. Lasting relationships require individuals to choose the other as their mate every single day.

Don't Give More than You are Getting

Commitment and relationships are exchanges. By definition, they are connections that require give and take. Compromise is the name of the game, but just as I stated it earlier, always remember your worth. The most valuable player tends to concede the least. Also realize value is subjective. I definitely want a partner of comparable worth, but no one is more important to me than me. Just the same, I desire my partner to be confident of their worth. The strongest commitments are formed between two people seeking companionship and partnership, not benefactors and beneficiaries.

I have a general rule of thumb for both my business and personal relationships. I do not commit or expect more than I am willing to give in exchange. When someone inquires exactly what I am bringing to the table, I gladly reply. I freely offer honesty, dedication, hard work, and quick wit. Many find it hard to match my quick wit, but I refuse to negotiate with another party that is unwilling or unable to match my hustle. Contracts or more than words scribed on a paper. Contracts represent executable power. Commitment is more than a simple promise or a vow. Commitment is an action word. The promise should be a reflection of an individual's behavior. If your partner is committed to the relationship, their actions should reflect thatdedication. If you are committed to your personal growth as a single individual, you have to invest the time and effort in making it so.

    I am committed to self-care. I am dedicated to improving comprehensive health. I am devoted to enabling women to discover their innermost desires and empowering them to embrace their sexuality. My devotion is born from a passion for healthcare. I am not satisfied with mediocrity or the status quo. I want people to thrive and excel. So I work hard to reach as many souls as I can. I want this message to catch like wildfire and consume the female community. I work hard to keep the conversation growing.

SEX AFTER...

CHAPTER 5: ...CHILDREN

Do not do yourself a disservice by skipping over this chapter because you do not and may not have any plans ever to physically give birth to a child. If you have ever given birth to an idea and come to the realization that something in this world is bigger than your personal being, I promise you can take something away from this message. Also, if you are considering having children, please take to heart this message before you start your journey.

At present, I find myself at this station in life. Being a physician, counselor, college educated and goal driven professional still did not fully prepare me for this particular challenge. In all the previous chapters I stress self-care, exploration, and pleasure mapping to acknowledge, discover, and fulfill your needs. Now, how do you stay committed to a seemingly selfish mission with one of the biggest responsibilities ever entrusted to any human being staring you in the face? Well, before I was garnered with the title of mother, I was privileged to be adorned with the title of physician. I have patients who entrust me with their health. In residency, I quickly realized why restrictions are placed on the hours young doctors are allowed to administer care to their patients. When you first put on that white coat, physically touch your patient, listen to their heartbeat and make that promise to do all you can in their best interest, even to your detriment, you find it difficult to leave your charge until each patient is safely returned home in good health. Still, no matter how hard I tried to fight it, my body taught me a valuable lesson: I am unable to offer my mental, physical, and emotional best without REST! Beyond self-preservation, I had to realize I owe it to my patients to make my own health and wellbeing a priority. When you are at your best, you can give your best to all of those who depend on you. You have a responsibility to take your best care of your being, including your sexual being.

I frequently fly across the country for both business and personal reasons. I have a tendency to ignore the standard public service announcement given by the dutiful flight attendants before the ascent of the aircraft into the clear blue skies. I am usually praying for safe travels and that no one ever have need to remember these lifesaving instructions. However, I encourage you to really listen to their requests. In regards to oxygen masks, the attendant always instructs parents to secure their own mask before fitting their child with oxygen. Prior to having my own child, I could easily intellectualize all the reasons why the adults would need to maintain their oxygen levels. Humans need oxygen for cognition and physical functions. But now as a parent who frequently takes flight with my child, I am hesitant. I truly wonder if, in that awful moment, I would put my mask on before my child.

On a recent flight while pondering this very thought, my own mother apparently read my mind. She informed me she would not put on her mask until I put on my mask. I did not find that piece of information helpful at all, because then I realized I have two people depending on me to breathe oxygen before they would breathe oxygen. As you might imagine, an argument ensued. A flight attendant appears to diffuse to the verbal discord of mother and daughter with a little reassurance and common sense. First she assured us we were seated in seats that could accommodate all three of us – grandmother, mother and grandchild. If the cabin pressure should change, three separate masks would drop down for our use. Furthermore, the flight attendant took notice of my toddler holding her bottle and gave us all a simple math lesson. She pointed out that my little girl had two hands, my mother had two hands, and I also had two hands. So there were six hands between the three of us. Even if we did not have confidence in the ability of small toddler hands, we still had four capable adult hands to place 3 masks. I immediately came to the conclusion that I can simultaneously use one hand to secure oxygen for my child and the other hand to secure oxygen for myself. However, my mom was not yet at ease. She said she needed three hands because she felt responsible for both her child and grandchild. So we agreed amongst ourselves that my mother and I would use our non-dominant left hands to grab our own oxygen masks and use our dominant right hands to secure the third mask on my child.

This single ordeal has taught me numerous life lessons that I am near giddy to share with you. First, you are already innately equipped with what you need to navigate any obstacle life throws at you. Secondly, know your abilities and don't take on more than you can handle. Thirdly, do not be so quick to turn down offered assistance. Lastly, and I hate to admit it, but mothers are usually right.

Remember Life Before the Baby

Life before my child could be defined as cycles of a self-consumed workaholic and a selfishly adventurous travel enthusiast. I would work all of my assigned shifts and had a second job on my days off. Over the course of a few months I would be near burn-out. Then I would schedule a vacation to rest and rejuvenate. However, I would never reallyrelax. I would enjoy traveling, sightseeing, wining and dining. It was so bad I would often return from vacation just as exhausted, if not more so, than before I left. It didn't take long for my body to show signs of neglect to my health. My blood pressure was on the rise. I would get frequent headaches. My menstrual cycle lost all signs of regularity. One night I returned home from the hospital and parked my car in the garage. Luckily I also turned off the engine before I fell asleep in my vehicle. I was too exhausted to even make it into the house to my bed. In hindsight, I realize pushing myself to that point of exhaustion could have been fatal. I could have fallen asleep at the wheel while driving. If I had left the engine in my car running, I would have exposed myself to lethal levels of carbon monoxide gas. So at that point, I realized I needed to get my work and personal life balance in order. I quickly discovered there was no instantaneous fix. I tried and failed more times than I care to count, but I eventually was able to carve out sufficient time to take a real break. After some time off, I had more energy to tackle my next challenge, which was my personal life.

As a carefree single person, my romantic and sexual entanglements came with a "for entertainment purposes only" disclosure statement. I was committed to having fun and seeking pleasure. While I had a desire to have children, it was not on my mind the night my daughter was conceived. So some of the first advice I give couples struggling to conceive is to stop trying. If you are already a parent or a workaholic, the same principles still apply. You must quit adding pressure to what should be a purely pleasurable experience. You have to allow a space for chemistry to flow, and stress is a roadblock to ecstasy. Even if your goal is not procreation, do not get distracted. Do not let thoughts of work, school, family dysfunction, or anything unrelated to carnal delight intrude on sexy time. You may never be as carefree as you once may have been before children, or even before your career. Nonetheless, you have to make personal life and your sex life a priority.

My work fulfills my desire to heal others and also fulfills my financial requirements to live the life I live. My family and friends fulfill my sense of belonging. They all give me the support and encouragement I need to be a good worker and in turn a good friend. My sex life fulfills one of my most primal carnal needs to just feel. It heightens my senses. After I climax and come apart in a million pieces, I have a newfound clarity to put the pieces back together. I am invigorated with anticipation to catalogue my next accomplishment. Being too tired for sex is nonsensical to me. Good sex is revitalizing. Challenge yourself to masturbate when you are beyond drained and tired at the end of the day. You may very well pass out into some of the deepest sleep just shy of a coma, and then awaken refreshed and energized.

A Bundle of Joy Comes with a Ball of Nerves

The one thing I miss most from my pre-parenthood days has to be sleep. I have and still occasionally watch my child sleep. As I take notice of her peaceful state, I too find solace in knowing she is healthy, safe and sound. Now any other time, I am just a ball of nerves. I wish someone had warned me that being a mother was literally nerve wracking. Whenever she is not in my presence,

I wonder if she is safe under a watchful eye. Worrying becomes second nature. But in all honesty, this obsessive worrying is not natural. You have to trust yourself and trust your instincts. I would never knowingly allow anyone who meant my child harm to be in her presence. Still, I struggle with time apart from by baby.

Here you have this little helpless human being that needs you for everything. So as a parent, you commit to fulfilling your obligations and providing those needs. These obligations of motherhood forced my sexual being into a leave of absence and almost early retirement. My pelvic floor had been reconfigured from carrying my bundle of joy. Then the physical and emotional toll of delivery further disassembled my sex. The joyous occasion didn't end in the hospital. Upon arriving home, I endured the mood swings and hormone roller coaster ride of a psychopath. I cried uncontrollably for absolutely no reason at all. I personally made the decision to sacrifice my lovely breasts for eight months. I hooked a vacuum pump to my nipples to extract milk andprovide nature's best nutrition. I had transformed into a dairy cow devoid of any sexual purpose or desire. I was overwhelmed with my duties as a mother and providing for an infant, but I was warped with determination to not fail my child. I would rationalize the need to go to work to provide for my family. However, I did not find it easy to separate from my child for much else. I didn't believe life existed outside of motherhood. My only purpose in life became meeting the needs of my child, so my needs went neglected. I allowed my asexual state to continue way too long, but the thought of pursing any form of pleasure or self-care seemed almost absurd. I lost confidence in my previous expert abilities to arouse myself and masturbate. I was literally scared to touch myself. While self-sacrifice for the wellbeing of your child is considered necessary and honorable, I think I went a little too far. I had lost my way. I could not see life beyond motherhood. My sex life was on life support and the coroner was getting ready to pronounce her expiration. I had to find the courage to start over.

Where did my G-Spot go?

I felt like a fumbling teenager all over again, but I had to relearn my anatomy. After pregnancy, you may need a refresher in anatomy. Remember a seven-to-ten pound watermelon stretched your pelvic floor to the max. Do not fret. Your musculature has a natural elasticity to assist in the much-needed snap-back. However, and to the surprise of many new mothers, nothing seems to be where you left it. And by nothing, I mean almost everything that brought you titillatinggratification. Rip up that old pleasure map. The landscape has definitely changed. I had to redraw my pleasure map. I will not lie. The process was frustrating. I had previously put a great deal of time and effort into learning and mastering my sexual blueprint to have it all ripped to shreds. So my first hurdle was coming to terms with the realization I would have to muster up the vigor to educate myself all over again.

Many believe that losing one of the five senses (sight, taste, smell, touch or hearing) will enhance the others. I found this narrative to be true one evening. While enjoying a long hot shower, the steam filled the space and visibility was nil. I couldn't see, but I felt every hot dribble of water on every inch of my body. I lathered my body with the most delicious smelling soap and my touch felt almost electric. Also mind you, this incident occurred almost eight months after the birth of my child and I had been completely devoid of any sexual encounters. I finally felt a wanting to try to find my missing erotic zones. I spread the lips of my vulva and allowed the water to wash over my clitoris and vulva. In the midst of baptizing my sex, those sorely missed feelings of the most erogenous kind came flooding back to mind. Emboldened with arousal, I spread my butt cheeks to the outpour of my steaming shower and slid my finger into my vaginal opening. Imagine my elation to my more posteriorly located, lost but now found, G-spot!

Please, do not be misled by the near tragic demise of my sexuality. I would do it all again in a heartbeat, but I would also be smarter. When you know better you do better. I now know to never neglect my sexual self. I would take advantage of those hormone surges. I would be sure to incorporate regular sexual activity into my daily routine to keep my pelvic muscles engaged. Most importantly, I would accept help when offered. At first, I did not want to talk to anyone about my troubles. I finally had an open conversation with my Obstetrician/Gynecologist. She assured me changes in my libido were normal, but also emphasized these changes should not be accepted as permanent.

Remember How You Made that Baby

I must take a moment to acknowledge the irony of post-parenthood sexual activity. Ask yourself, how does a little baby, being a byproduct of sex, become the largest hurdle to sex? Sex creates babies, and babies hinder sex. Fight the irony! You have to remember how you made that baby. If you feel you have lost your way and your memory, I suggest you consider a few proven techniques to treat amnesia. Cognitive therapy involves exercises aimed at mental recall. You need to recreate familiar space and conditions that jog your memory. Every new mom deserves a date night. Revisit activities and hobbies you previously enjoyed.

Increasing physical activity has fourfold benefits: Exercise improves cognition, health, appearance, and confidence. There are specific exercises to get your core engaged, hips realigned and that pelvic floor tight and right. I propose you do an Internet search for post-baby workouts. Set daily goals to do squats, crunches, and pelvic thrusts until you feel the burn. Just remember it took you nine months to bake that bun in the oven, so weight will not melt away nor will muscles tighten up overnight. I doubt you made the baby alone, so get your mate involved. Reconnect with new realistic goals. Life will never be the same, but different does not have to mean less fulfilling. You must invest some well-deserved time in yourself and your relationships to get the results you want and be the parent your child deserves.

We are all born sexual beings who are birthed from the sex organs of a woman. You are a testament to the fact that your parents, grandparents, great grandparents, and so on were all at one point getting it on. My maternal grandmother had fourteen children, so I assume she was having her fair share of sexual activity. Unfortunately, I am not aware if she actually enjoyed sex. I am not even sure if my grandmother was aware that she should enjoy sex. So now one of my self-appointed missions in life is to make sure every woman is aware of her certain indubitable right to be pleased.

Life Just Got Bigger Than You

My first day in the hospital as a licensed physician, I went without sleep for more than 36 hours until every single patient assigned to my charge was in stable condition. The first day I brought my baby girl home I lost just as much sleep. The first time I held my daughter in my hands, I knew I would give my life to ensure her safety. So many times I had to come to terms with the life lesson that there are things bigger than my own mere existence. In these moments I am humbled. I have to take time to remember how far I have come in my career, life's journey, and womanhood.

I found great solace and solidarity in motherhood once I found the courage to confide in my friends who had faced many similar challenges. We swapped so many stories about some of the most embarrassing and beautiful maternity moments. I wish I would have known in the beginning that my bundle of joy could kick my bladder without warning and cause a grown woman to piss her pants. I had not wet my pants since I was a toddler, yet there I stood in my living room saturated. Well, it all made for good practice to change my own diapers before the bundle of joy arrived. Sometimes, I could just laugh until I cry.

You should also take a moment to recall all the obstacles you have already overcome in life to be in your current space. Children are not to be seen as obstacles, but blessings that make us desire better lives. You have to believe in your abilities to improve your current situation. Acknowledge you deserve all the good that comes to you. My mom has told me my entire life I can do whatever I set my mind to do. She would encourage me when I wanted to give up and tell me I was going to be an excellent physician. She very well may have had ulterior motives. My mother's retirement plan had great stakes in my success. Throughout my pregnancy, my mother constantly offered assurance that I would also be a great mom. I am so glad my mother is usually right about almost everything. I am even more grateful she was able to retire and help me raise my child.

The birth of a child tends to birth an overpowering desire in even the most flawed individual to be a perfect parent. Striving for this form of excellence, I am sorry to say, can be disheartening and exhausting. I advise any new parent to forget perfection and instead focus on living in the moment. Babies only stay babies for what feels like a split second. They grow so fast. They learn and you get to experience something new every day. You do not want to miss these moments. When you are in your child's presence, do everything in your power to be present. Still, you owe it to yourself to maintain a since of self apart from motherhood. The best advice I have ever gotten in life as a career professional and a mother would be to continue getting better at being myself. My child deserves to know the most self-assured and fulfilled me that I can be.

SEX AFTER...

CHAPTER 6: ...BETRAYAL

Set the stage and scene of your autobiographical Greek tragedy. Only you know the specific players and sequence of events in your devastating, personal production. Unfortunately, every woman knows the disappointment of betrayal and deception. Was it infidelity? Did you endure some form of horrible trauma? Whatever or whomever dealt you those cards of deceit, I beseech you to declare this time and space for healing. You may never forget, but the goal is forgiveness. You have to forgive the offender. You have to let go of the anger and negative energy this person provokes in your spirit. It stains your aura and dims your light. You also have to forgive yourself. You are never responsible for another person's bad actions. So banish the thought that you allowed someone to violate your being.

I have lost count of the times I have been lied to by enemies in friends' clothing and lovers who seem to only love themselves. I have been disappointed by people who swore undying love and by foes who dare not hide their hate, all the same. I have learned to not wallow in the pool of disenchantment and regret.

Instead, I let it wash off and leave the puddle behind. I do not mean to give the impression that pardoning these transgressions is an easy or simple process. However, it becomes a little less loathsome when you have done the work and you know your worth. These undeserving individuals and deplorable events have less mattering to a self-assured and satisfied woman aware of her value and abilities.

In my early twenties, one of my closest confidants revealed her true motives for befriending me. I was heartbroken to hear from her own deceptive lips the intentions to derail my success and undermine my self-confidence all because of her earnest belief that she deserved the life I had been blessed to live. This woman was someone I had known since grade school. I had shared with her some of my deepest convictions and sacred secrets. So you can imagine how her duplicity rocked me to the core. She was not only a liar, but a thief, who stole my innocence. I naively put my faith in the code of sisterhood. I believed women were nurturers, and we shared a common goal to support other women and lift each other up. This unwritten sacred rule of womanhood has been forever tarnished by her actions.Moreover, I wasted years trying to rationalize her disloyalty. Why would she want to orchestrate my downfall? What could I have done to a person to garner this type ofanimosity? You would think with all this trifling person took away from my life, she would at least given me some answers. I wanted so badly to know her logic it threatened my own sanity. I thought I had to understand her reasoning to come to my own resolution and get closure. But now I know, my closure was never hers to give.

Presently, her betrayal seems trivial in the comparison to the real traumatic experiences so many women continue tosuffer at hands of friends and strangers alike. I am referring to sexual trauma, abuse, and assault. These travesties represent betrayal of the worse kind. I must admit the limitations of my platform to address the complexity of such a violation. I encourage any woman who has been victimized to report these criminal acts and seek professional advocates for counseling and support. This journey is not meant for you to travel alone. I do hope I can assist in initiating the healing process. Healing is truly a process and not an immediate destination. It takes work, sacrifice, and determination to possess your healing and wholeness.

Grieve the Loss of Trust

Betrayal is a violation of trust that leaves you with a loss. Grieving that loss is a necessary process and the first step to healing. Your first reaction may be anger, and it is a natural, primal emotion. Your anger is warranted and justified, but you must not allow yourself to stagnate in your feelings of hurt and mistrust. Do not become a mirror of everything you despise. The biggest falsehood to hinder progression from anger is the belief that we are unable to control our emotions. As human beings, we are designed to feel, but you are not defined by your feelings. Be angry, but not an angry woman. Be mad, but not a mad man. At your core, you are a decent human being that encountered unfortunate circumstance that triggered a reaction, an emotion. So you dig deep down into your core values and drive out anger with love. Love yourself enough to want to restore everything that treacherous thief stole from you. Do not wait for anyone to give you anything, but instead reach out and take it. You have undeniable rights to sanity and peace of mind. Take back your peace of mind. Take back your confidence. Take back your security.

While living in southeast Washington DC, my car was broken into a few times. One particular time, a thief broke my car window and stole my radio. Of course, I called the cops. I was angry and frustrated, and this officer showed up asking a million questions. I did not know the answers to most of his questions. I did know that someone had taken what belonged to me, and I wanted it back, immediately. In that moment I could do nothing to hide my annoyance. So the officer acknowledged my tones of exasperation, but went on to inform me that his inquiries were necessary to file a report. Straightway, his remarks struck a nerve with me, because on the surface it appeared we had two different agendas. I was the victim of a crime, and I wanted the criminal brought to justice. He seemed to be primarily focused on his policies, procedures, and paperwork. So then I had a question for the policeman. I wanted to know how his report was going to get me closer to restitution. Unbeknownst to me, this well-informed patrolman was more than prepared to drop some knowledge and help me adjust my attitude.

The police officer went on to explain that his report needed to be comprehensive and specific in order to be compared to other robberies and infractions in the area. Motives and patterns have been considered just as identifying as fingerprints with serial criminals. Thus he wanted to do a thorough job to increase the probability of catching the thief that stole my property and restoring my sense of security. Furthermore, in regards to my restitution, the insurance company would also require his tedious report to open a claim to repair my vehicle.

That police officer imparted to me a couple of lessons in criminology and anger management. Beyond simply acknowledging the crime and criminal, you need to take a detailed account of patterns and behavior. Whoever violated your trust or broke your confidence warrants a thorough recollection of their past behaviors. This activity is not about them, but to help you recognize those patterns in the future. You never want to let another scandalous offender pull the wool over your eyes and jeopardize your wellbeing. Revisit the pain caused and catalogue all the infidelity. Then, file your report in hopes that you will recognize future patterns of behavior. You owe it to yourself and other victims to report criminal behavior to the proper authorities.

I realize it is difficult to come to terms with the fact you may never know a person's motive to defraud you. My curiosity has unfortunately been at the root of quite a bit of mental anguish. I really had to force myself to reconcile my inquisition of the unknown to be in vain. Sometimes we just make the simplest thing the most complex problems. Bad people do bad things. I had to accept that deplorable behavior alone defines despicable individuals. I do not need to know your motives. You do not need to know the reasons. You just need to know the facts and push forward. Do not let curiosity derail your progress. I never got my car radio back. I am not aware if the offender was ever caught, but the report was filed. I filed my insurance claim, and I got another radio. Unfortunately, most transgressions are not so simply resolved. I wish they were, but it takes time.

Not right away, but I did soon realize that after listening to the officer's response to my vexed disposition, my anger had dissipated. He matched my flippant brashness with proficient knowledge of how to accomplish his task. The goal of grieving after you have been violated is to ultimately resolve those feelings of resentment, inadequacy, and loss in order to move past the hurt. It is not simple. It is a process. Success requires knowledge of where you are and where you are trying to go. Gather your facts, recount the transgressions, and resolve to know and do better.

Please Don't Shut Up or Shut Down

Vaginismus is a pain disorder of the vagina. Your vagina physically shuts down and any form of penetration becomes painful and intolerable. Women who suffer from vaginismus are unable to insert tampons and often incapable of tolerating pelvic exams by their physician, let alone penetrative intercourse. This condition is caused by both emotional and physical triggers. Most commonly the triggering event is related to trauma. The symptoms of this disorder can range from mild intolerance to significantly debilitating. As daunting as this diagnosis may appear, there are treatments and vaginismus is curable.

A multi-faceted treatment plan aimed at physical rehabilitation and cognitive therapy to resolve the emotional and physical triggers are imperative. Education and counseling can direct patients toward recovery. Physical rehabilitation may require consultation with a physical therapist or trained healthcare provider familiar with pelvic floor conditioning and vaginal dilators. Vaginal dilators are plastic or silicone cylinders that are manufactured in varying sizes to gradually dilate the vaginal vault. They are not vibrators or stimulators. These tools are inserted very slowly and methodically into the vagina to gradually stretch the contracted walls of the vagina. This gradual dilations is aimed at eventually allowing a person who suffers from vaginismus to tolerate some degree of penetration. I recommend this therapy only be deployed under the direction of a physician, physical therapist, or sex therapist. Physically dilating the vagina needs to be accompanied with cognitive behavioral therapy to address the emotional triggers that cause vaginismus.

Often after betrayal and trauma, we tend to withdraw into a personal cocoon of safety and security. We may unintentionally shut out those who genuinely want to help us recover. No one wants to recount all the details of disappointment, which leads many to stop talking altogether. We lose our voice, but we cannot remain silent. We have to speak up and tell our story. Our testimonies could save another fromtreachery. Also, pent up and unresolved resentment can poison your psyche while the culprit that betrayed your trust lives on in ignorant bliss. Do not surrender that kind of power to a thief! Take back your peace of mind by speaking your mind. Do not be afraid to accept help, and tell your close loved ones what you need from them to recover your sense of self.

Restore Your Sense of Self

Restoration means to be made whole. When these flawed human beings let you down and break you down, you are left to pick up the pieces and make yourself whole. In order to restore order to your brokenness, you are going to have to give yourself permission to be selfish. You are going to have to devise a plan to reclaim everything that has been taken from you.

When that woman dishonored our friendship I lost confidence in the goodness of humanity and the solidarity of sisterhood. I had also lost someone I thought was a good friend. I was never one to have a large quantity of close friends, but did have quality friends. But when faced with adversity I often found solace in the company of family. I come from a very large southern family. I was raised by some phenomenal women. My grandmother, mother, and aunts were a group of strong-willed, accomplished women who taught me integrity and discipline. Still, none one of them could be considered saints. These women were flawed, but I never questioned their love for me. Most of my aunts were not college educated but they constantly pushed me to achieve higher education. These women encouraged me with words and deeds. They all made it crystal clear they wanted me and the entire next generation of my family to be better than the preceding generation. I concluded that to avoid the hurt I had endured, I needed to acquire friends who strongly resembled my family.

When that scoundrel stole my radio, I called in the proper authorities to file a report. Again, criminal infractions need to be reported to law enforcement. Assault and trauma can create deep wounds that need professional attention to assist restoration. The abuse has physical and emotional recourse. Betrayal and trauma hurts. The deceits cuts like a knife. The stress wreaks havoc on your sanity. Your feelings hurt. Your body hurts. Even your spirit may be wounded. If you are suffering from physical ailments like abrasions or broken bones, you know you need medical attention. You present yourself to the emergency room or doctor's office to be bandaged. Your mental anguish is not easily recognized by the naked eye, but you have to be in tune to your psyche. You know when you are suffering with emotional and mental unrest. Counseling and therapy can equip you with the tools and insight to resolve those inner struggles. Mental health professions are diversely skilled individuals that provide a service for your fractured psyche similar to the care medical professionals provide for your physical wounds. Rehabilitation is possible and there are so many people who have accepted a calling in life to shoulder the burden on those who need the assistance. Most religious sects provide some form of counseling. There are various support groups and hotlines for trauma. Reach within for the strength to reach out to all of the hands waiting to help you heal.

Sex is Off the Table

There are only a few circumstances where I will not advocate for emboldened sexuality. Sexual trauma happens to be one of thoseinstances. Some victims have attempted to mask their pain with hyper-sexuality. Our coping mechanisms need to focus on healing and restoring a state of peace. Betrayal, trauma and abuse have lengthy roads to recovery. There is no simple fix. For this reason, sex needs to be off the table until the healing process has begun. I urge self-exploration, not of your sex, but your wounds. Identify each physical and mental impairment. Do not bandage it to cover thedeformity or blemish, but bandage your lesions to keep them protected and clean to promote healing. Brace your brokenness to restore stability to your weakness. My brace, or support, begins with my faith and my family. Both my faith and my family have seen me through some difficult times. Their love is unconditional and provides a much needed safe space. Where is your safe space? You have to find that place where you can feel secure even with your ailments and deformities. I still believe you have everything you need in your own person to resolve and restore your life from traumatic happenings, but you still may need momentary support from others to gather the strength to find your inner abilities to heal.

I also do not recommend a permanent celibacy. If betrayal or trauma stole your mojo, you have every right to take it back. I just want it to come back on your terms and only when you are ready. Early in this chapter, anger was addressed. Now more importantly, fear needs to be purged from yourconsciousness. Once you have experienced the pain of betrayal or trauma, it is only natural to be afraid of getting hurt again. Acknowledge your fear and reservation, but do not become a person limited by your emotions. You have been injured and may be scared, but you are more than anger and fear. You are love and courage. You are resilient. You will overcome this hurdle just as you have others, all in due time.

Set the Table Again

Restarts are so refreshing to me. I try to remember to restart my phone regularly. I frequently am forced to restart my computer when it malfunctions. I have come to terms with the fact my life, especially my sex life, can also benefit from the occasional restart. To start again is to learn again and live again. Fresh starts start at the beginning. Revisit your pleasure map and explore your anatomy, appreciating every scar. Scars are not blemishes, but instead think of these markings as evidence of healing. Stretch marks are not indicative of deformity, but of resilience. You are a multifaceted work of art. Every mark, wound, and lesion has made you an ever more unique specimen of beauty to be adored. Your physical appearance should be revered as a thing of beauty under any circumstances.

My career has taken me to places I never dreamed I would be. I have sat at the heads of tables and amongst field leaders whom I previously idolized. Just the same, I have been in situations where I was forced to share space with people who had previously betrayed my trust and caused me heartbreak. Luckily, I have had the good fortune to always look amazing.

I am confident that my haters are watching, so I am sure to give them a good show. The best revenge is to live your life without regret. Accomplish every dream you so desire despite every voice that said you never would or could. Betrayal is an unfortunate but common stop on the train tracks of life. However you better not let it derail you. You have to continue with forward progress. The only way to achieve and accomplish anything worth having will require you to conjure your inner strength to push pass frustration and disappointment.

You are worthy of love and respect, so demand it. Demand everything you want and need. With that being said, set the table in the presence of your friends and foes. Not everyone you interact with will wish you well. Despite their presence in your common space, I challenge you to thrive. Walk, talk, look, sound, and appear your best, even if you have to fake it until you make it to your defined destination of success. Everyone has a story, but none like the one you have lived to tell. Do not forget that you are indeed still alive. That horrific, treacherous lie of the enemy did not kill you, but made you stronger. Show everyone who is watching your strength and power.

SEX AFTER...

CHAPTER 7: ...DIVORCE

If you hope this chapter will tell you how right you were to dump your partner because you deserve better, please accept my apologies now. I am not here to insert myself into domestic disputes. I am here to speak to the audience of women who have already come to terms with the demise, or expiration, of their marriage. I have no interest in rehashing who may be to blame. In all honesty, all parties have to carry a portion of blame. It takes at least two parties to commit to marriage, and those same parties are again responsible for the likeminded departure and end to the union. I do not possess the authority to absolve you of any culpability. I am, however, very capable of questioning your sanity. If you are no longer getting what you need from any situation, you may need to consider a change. Remember, you already have innate abilities to fulfill your every need. Staying in an unfulfilling, unsatisfying relationship does not define loyalty, but insanity. Insanity is the only explanation for repeated actions with the expectation of different results. So again I ask, are you insane?

Now I dare not give the impression that every day should be sunshine, chocolates and roses. Unrealistic expectations of marriage are a common cause of divorce. Still, marriage should be to your benefit and not your detriment. If you are hoping to plot the course to your personal state of bliss, I very well may be able to assist you with that expedition. I want your divorce to be a happy transition to gratification and fulfillment of the sexual kind. I want you to be satisfied at this station in life. I want to remind you just how desirable and well suited you already are for thriving success. I want you to become everything you need and more. Then, and only then, should you consider future companionship. Two halves of two people do not a couple make. Only two whole persons can unite as a fulfilled couple.

Before we can get to that happy place we have to acknowledge we have lost something. Divorce has a unique grieving process. People associate bereavement with death, but really it has to do with any deficiency, absence, or loss. You are sorrowful and saddened by the loss of a loved one, not just when they die, but also when they are absent. Sometimes that absence may be due to illness, such as Alzheimer's dementia or even substance abuse. Both dementia and substance abuse can rob a person of their cognitive functions and consciousness. These people are no longer their true selves. They are the products of their illness. You must lament the absence of the person you remember and loved. Similarly with the end of marriage, your partner is no longer present in the capacity in which he or she vowed to be forever. You should mourn the loss.

Feelings of remorse and regret are natural. Most people do not get married with plans to get divorced, but it stills happen more times that anyone wants to admit. Divorce rates are on the rise in this country. You know that divorce is becoming way too common when divorce parties are now marketed events on websites for wedding planners. In conversation, I hear others refer to an individual, not on their second marriage, but on their third divorce. I am not here to judge, because to be divorced puts you in good company. You are definitely not alone. My hope is that once you bounce back from one divorce, I can lend you a few tools to recognize patterns and behaviors. Everyone can learn from their mistakes with a goal in mind to not repeat bad behavior. Primarily, I want you to feel confident with your aptitude in meeting your own needs. Then if you choose to seek another mate, I want you to also be assured you are equipped to choose wisely. Before you jump back on the horse and date the masses, first you should date you. You more than likely need a reintroduction to yourself, because we as women are constantly evolving and adjusting to life and circumstances. These traits are what make us uniquely beautiful, like the metamorphosing butterfly. I want you to date yourself to get to know what you like and don't like. I want you to be the world's best authority on everything *you*. When you know all there is to know about yourself, you will know what you need. This information is vital to assist you in properly identifying a companion that does not need to complete you, but adequately complements you.

Beginning Again

Starting over should be seen as another opportunity to get it right. Even if you feel you did it right the first time, starting again can be your chance to do it even better. My mom always taught me to rarely use shortcuts, and always start at the beginning. In the beginning, before you were married, there was a young lady or a little girl. In our youth, we were dreamers. Do you remember your youthful aspirations? I wanted to be a well-travelled hair stylist. I wanted a vacation home on the beach. I encourage you to really recklessly abandon your inhibitions and revisit the whimsical fancies of your youth. Your dreams are a glimpse into your heart's desires. Dreaming is how the unattainable becomes attainable. I do not mean the material things, but unearth your deepest desires and what makes you happy. Just a few years ago I fantasized about my routine journaling becoming a bestselling piece of literature. My daydreaming allowed me to discover my desire to share something with the world. First I had a vision, and then I aspired to make that dream come true. I set goals, deadlines, and actually had to do the work to complete the transformation from fantasy to reality. You are reading one of my wildest dreams.

I am not only referring to the words on a page. You are reading my longing to be comfortable with my self-defined sexuality and my current confidence in the expression of my sex. I still aspire to achieve unimaginable, carnal blessedness. Do you dream about orgasms? Do you dream about multiple, soul-stirring inner eruptions of pleasure? You should. Your dreams are going to give you a road map to true happiness and your purpose on this planet. Once you know your purpose you can work towards honing your gifts and sharing your talent. After you give of yourself to the world, you have to pour back into your spirit. I believe sex is a part of that spiritual essence. Your health is the working mechanics of your mind, body and spirit. If you wish for peace of mind, I implore you to heal any trauma, decrease stress, and meditate on your betterment. If you long for a beautiful physique and clean bill of health, you should start exercising, eat clean, and seek instruction from your healthcare professional. If you seek spiritual wellbeing, you need to feed your soul with positivity, stay true to your core values, and embrace your sex. I cannot stress enough the importance of total self-care that includes all three elements.

What have you neglected to do for yourself? Remember circumstances, such as divorce, that force change also allow opportunities for us to do things differently, or even better. This time is your chance to put yourself first, at least for a moment. Now I want you to take those long since filed away and indefinitely postponed items on your overlooked agenda and set some goals. If you never got your passport, you have one week to complete the application process. How else will you travel the world? It really is just that simple. Step by step, conquer all those small obstacles that keep you from your big dreams.

Learn Your Lesson

We are all flawed individuals, and some more so than others. Nonetheless, divorce should make you much more aware of what you are *not* looking for in a mate. It is important to know what traits you do not desire in a mate. So many times I hear people recount various clues they seemingly missed in hindsight. Oftentimes we fail to walk away from our known deal breakers. For the life of me, I am unable to discern why we habitually excuse bad behavior and then find ourselves in utter disbelief and bewildered by the sociopath we allow to share our space. Please take note that I use inclusive pronouns. I have many times questioned my need to be committed after I find myself in a committed relationship with a crazy person. In my twenties I apparently had no foresight, only hindsight. It was only after the relationship had ended tragically that I could suddenly recognize my partner's peculiar patterns of behavior. I wish we, as women, would never settle for anything less than all the goodness we truly deserve. I do not ever want you to sell yourself short. I want you to know your value so you can demand your worth.

Yes, I have had my fair share of relationships. As lovers and friends have come and gone, I find comfort in my proficiency to skillfully navigate my pleasure points. I must also confess, I have had a few reliable battery operated companions that take good direction. My trusty vibrator is a useful tool for electrifying stimulation. I need to dispel some common misconceptions about vibrators and sex toys in general. Sex toys are not specifically for lonely spinsters with lacking sex lives. Actually, a vibrator is of little use if you are unaware of the locations that need stimulation. They may be used to massage and discover unexplored erotic zones. However, vibrators and stimulators are best used in experienced hands that already have existing knowledge of their own pleasure zones. Sex toys are meant to enhance your sex life, thus making them ideal for sexually apt singles and couples alike. Many women fear a common falsehood that these sex toys can actually over-stimulate and decrease sensations, and ultimately make achieving orgasms without the use of stimulators difficult. Again, these concerns are unfounded. Stimulators can increase vaginal secretions that serve as natural lubricants and augment sensitization. The regular stimulation can also increase the intensity of your climax.

Make no mistake, vibrators and stimulators are not replacements for desired companionship, just as dating applications on your smartphone are not substitutes for good judgment and common sense. When you take the time to indulge in self-pleasure, you avoid the many mishaps of desperation. You need to be fulfilled and of sound mind. Equip yourself with the time and knowledge to make wise decisions. Remember, you are not insane. You will not repeat previous actions that brought you undesirable results.

Make Your Next Move Your Best Move

When I am dating, I have no tolerance for dishonesty. You get one opportunity to disappoint me before I will cut you off. I do not let people lie to me repeatedly. I am a firm believer that you should do whatever you say you are going to do. Some might say I am hard on everybody about keeping their word but do not hold myself to the same statute. Apparently I lie to myself all the time, seemingly without much consequence. I tell myself I am going to take time off, get a massage or treat myself. Every week I promise to improve my diet starting Monday morning. I will indulge in at least one piece of candy and abandon my adopted healthy lifestyle adaptation by lunchtime. All the same, almost every Friday evening after I complete the working week, I promise to take it easy on the weekend and do something just for me. I rarely completely abandon my work obligations. Every so often, I do manage to get in a little self-indulgence, but not to the extent I pledged. It has come to the point where I really have to ask myself why I accept my own empty promises. Yet I still have not given up or cut myself off. I still believe I am going to change. I want change. I want to do better. I have failed myself. I have come to know disappointment and failure at my very own hands, but I still have hope. I have faith in my strong will and desire to accomplish every aspiration my heart and mind can conjure.

I am getting better and better at dating myself, so my next companion will have some pretty large shoes to fill. It appears my good behavior is constantly being rewarded. The better I treat myself, the more the universe reciprocates my efforts with good company. From friendships to business relationships, I now have the good fortune to gravitate towards and attract those who want to bestow more profitable business ventures and stimulating companionship into my life. It is truly amazing what can happen when you put your best foot forward. However, you will find it very hard to drive forward while constantly looking in the rearview mirror. While it is very important to know and remember historic mistake and events to avoid repetition, you do not want to get stuck in the past. Look forward and live forward.

SEX AFTER...

CHAPTER 8: ...FAILURE

Failure hurts. However, I accept it is a necessary obstacle to success. What is failure? I think of failure as the opportunity to edit a masterpiece. If you have never failed, then you must have never tried. I find one of the best teachers in life is a good fall on your hind parts. Once you experience the smarting pain of your own shortcomings, I am confident you will be motivated to work even harder to avoid future flops, disappointments, and bankruptcy.

I know failure. For as much success as I have had in my academic career, I have a lengthy list of failed examinations, declined applications, and missed opportunities. I have aborted many missions because I knew the end result would be bankruptcy and debt. I have lost more money than I have found. I have to work really hard for every penny earned. I remember every pitfall, barricade, and landmine in order to not encounter that road hazard again. As painful as the process may be, you need to recognize failure and study it. This practice will prevent you from recurrent setbacks on your road to success.

You Won't Know Success Until You Fail

Let me preface this next story for those who have longstanding, tumultuous relationships with mathematics. Do not dwell on the numbers, but please receive the message. While I was in medical school, I had the pleasure of dating a few professional athletes. These men were very impressed with my knowledge of most sports. So we would discuss their personal and team statistics. In one particular game, a shooting guard made 18 of 29 attempted shots in a basketball game. So I calculated his shooting average to be 62% (18/29= 62%). On my school's grading scale that would have correlated with an "F." However, I was wrong. That was a career high for this young man. Those 18 shots earned him 39 points for his team and ultimately a victory. Right off I learned that the same numbers carry a different value and currency depending on the situation. In sports, it appears that the bar had been set extremely low. I sure wish my schools had been on a similar grading scale as the athletic statisticians! I also learned the value of just trying. Imperfectly, this shooter attempted 29 shots. When he missed, it only counted as 1 missed opportunity to score. Conversely, when he scored, the shot counted for 1, 2, or even 3 points. So even though he only successfully connected with 18 shots, these shots multiplied into 39 points.

After such a successful night on the court, this high scoring sharp shooter was more than confident he would also be scoring between the sheets. However, my plans that evening only consisted of intense preparation for a comprehensive examination. With school still in session, I went on to teach him yet another valuable lesson in life. Career success and all the money in the world would not buy him happiness or sweet carnal bliss the night before an exam. In turn, he taught this honor student a lesson in life. I learned that girls who would not put out, also would not get free tickets to All Star Weekend. We both learned a lot.

Again, the most important lessoned I took away from that laughable strikeout session would have to be the little cost of trying. You do not have to score with every shot attempt, but when you do, the points are more than worth it. Also the more you try creates more opportunity. You will have more opportunity to make it count. Just the same, you are also more likely to miss a few. Still, when the game is all over and the points are added, only the silly medical student is concerned with how many shots you miss. The news will only print the points scored and the game victory.

No one is pining away to publish all of their failures. The billionaire will not voluntarily release the tax returns that reveal squandered millions, or even billons. The billionaire only erects skyscraping monuments of success to show the world. I surely do not want to show people all of my numerical and letter grades in physical chemistry. I am not going to volunteer all of my academic transcripts. However, every degree I earned hangs in my office. My successes in life are the result of many attempts and yes, even failures.

Psychology of Sexuality

Sexuality, success, and failure are all apart of human nature. However, I have found it difficult for all three to harmoniously dwell in the same space. When a person has a mindset of failure, he or she will be less likely to embrace their sexuality. I guess what I am really trying to say is that no one has ever described failure as sexy. But I think failure breeds determination and persistence. I do think those characteristics are sexy. I am very grateful for those overzealous lovers who were not deterred by my repeated rebuffs in the name of playing hard to get. Their unrelenting efforts to get close to me were endearing. I also found it reaffirmed how I am most definitely worth the effort. Whatever keeps you trying, even if you have been denied, must be worth every attempt.

Beyond the act of having sex, your sexuality is interconnected with your sense of self. Sex-positive individuals have positive self-image, faith in their abilities to hurdle obstacles, and ultimately a drive to succeed. Sex-assertive people consistently see sex as a possibility. No, I am not saying as a sex-assertive woman I constantly seek out every opportunity to masturbate or engage a partner for intercourse. My assertiveness is just as reliable as my watch. I remain in a predictable state pleasure seeking. Again, I am not always horny. My pleasure does not solely come from sex. I am very goal-oriented and receive great pleasure from accomplishing my given tasks. So now hopefully you can visualize the connection. Because I am very comfortable with my sexuality, which defines a large part of who I am as a woman, I am my own champion for what I desire and want from life. I have a passion for success, and a disdain for failure, and these emotions drive me to act accordingly. I work hard at attempts to satisfy my appetite to advance and avoid disappointment.

Remove "Can't" from Your Vocabulary

When you first picked up this book, I am sure your limited sexual repertoire led you to believe you could not evolve into a beautiful sexual butterfly. Yet here you are today. If you are not already a blossoming goddess of sexual energy, I am sure you are well on your way. You can and you will masterfully masturbate to the land of carnal bliss. You can and you will tease and titillate your partner into sexual submission. Whatever you desire to be and achieve is possible. Never give voice to any inabilities. You will encounter obstacles and roadblocks. In those instances you need to learn how to detour and still arrive at the desired destination.

I will use sex as an example. I talk about what I know. If you are not having the quantity or quality of sex you crave, the first step is to clearly identify the opposition. Why are you not having more sex? In order to engage in the act of having sex you need time, space, and participants. No one has been successful at adding more than the allotted 24 hours to each day. Time constraints require prioritizing and scheduling the time you need to get whatever you want. If you want it bad enough, wake up or go to bed a half an hour earlier or later, respectively. As for space, feel free to get creative. The possibilities are endless. Both of my sets of grandparents procreated while raising more than ten children in homes less than a thousand square feet. In the present day you have cars, enclosed garages, master bathrooms, washrooms, dens, man caves, and more. Find a closet somewhere. Make room or get a room. Participants are a non-issue to masterful masturbators. If you need your mate or partner, you both are going to have to get in sync. You have to communicate your desires, availability, and flexibility in order to find common ground. Compromise is a necessity. Maybe you can whisk your lover away on a romantic getaway to create the time and space you need. When a trip is not immediately feasible, steal away to your secret meeting space for a quick rendezvous. Quickies can be an exciting solution for those couples with tight schedules and multiple demands on their availability.

There will be times in life that limit the quantity of sexual encounters, but I do believe you can always find a solution. Now when it comes to quality, I never encourage compromising the quality of even the quickest of quickies. Make it the best three minutes of your day. First, I need to know exactly how you define good sex. Are you getting what you require to be aroused and satisfied? What are you expecting to feel and what are you actually experiencing? Many times our expectations set us up for failure. I have been told that those who set their expectations low are rarely disappointed. However, I am a firm believer in reaching for the stars. I encourage hope, eager anticipation and suspense. I also know your work ethic needs to match your expectancy to achieve exceptional results. Are you willing to work at getting the sex you desire?

Nowhere to Go but Up

Your sexuality and psyche are very closely intertwined. I know positive sexual energy motivates me. I feel great, thus I perform at a higher level. I credit a good deal of my career success to my personal success and evolving sexuality that defines my sense of self. My confidence has grown with my bolstered sense of sexuality. I have a very good memory. Surely, I have come a long way from that naïve, sexually suppressed and anorgasmic college freshman who set out on the epic journey to find herself. I presently stand now, more than just comfortable in my own skin, but terribly smitten with myself! I dare not lead you to believe my transformation was without turmoil. Everyone has hiccups.

I remember as a child when I would suffer with hiccups, my family would suggest all kinds of bizarre remedies. They would tell you to hold your breath for ten seconds or more. Some say you can scare hiccups away. One time my brother told me I had to drink a gallon of water. I would try anything because the involuntary spasms were so uncomfortable to me. I would not give up until the hiccups subsided. I really doubt any of my antics cured me. I think time just passed and so did the spasms. The moral of the story is still to never stop trying. I think I just may be too stubborn not to succeed. Even after I fail, I believe I can recover and conquer whatever task my heart so desires.

I will not accept failure as defeat. Many people think of failure as the end to whatever they had dreamed to accomplish. I do not think of failure as a finite destination at all. It is only a temporary status. I believe failure is the starting point of upward mobility. In order to go up you have to begin at a lower level. Also, I will not accept mediocrity. I refuse to believe I was only born to exist in commonplace, doing odd jobs with average, ordinary people. I am certain my ordained purpose in life will be fulfilled when I strive for excellence in the company of extraordinary people. I am even more self-assured that my animated and emboldened sexuality will propel me far past my wildest dreams of satisfaction. There really is nowhere to go but up.

SEX AFTER...

CHAPTER 9: ...MENOPAUSE

No one ever has time to properly plan a good midlife crisis when they really need one. I think certain unpredictable life changing events would be better received if they had the good manners to make an appointment. Just imagine how convenient it would be if you received a nice little invitation and RSVP card for menopause. You should think of "the change of life" as a festive event worthy of celebration and libations because it is indeed a milestone in womanhood. I look forward to menopause in the same manner that I anticipate retirement. When I retire, I will give up a title, an office, and my doctor's parking space, but I will also give up my obligations, duties and time constraints that keep me from the people and activities I love. Menopause is the retirement of your ovaries. You forfeit your fertility, and the job description of your reproductive organs definitely changes. However, you are still a sexual being. You do not have to sacrifice your sexual desire or satisfaction. You can abandon the responsibility of fertility and embrace a newfound sexual liberation. Also when I retire from my practice of medicine, I will still keep my Doctorate of Medicine. Menopausal women are still women. Moreover, these are women who should have garnered a certain sexual aptitude that not even menopause can take away. Try your best not to get bogged down with thoughts of loss, and focus instead on the much-deserved liberties granted in the prime of your sexual life span.

The More Things Change, the More Nothing Stays the Same

I want you to really understand menopause and the changes that come along with the experience. This change and transition in life has very few constants and consistencies. Menopause can commence as early as your thirties, or as late as your sixties. The unpredictability of normalcy makes it essential for every woman to be in tune with her body and state of wellness. When you know the normal, you are more likely to also recognize the abnormal. One of the first signs of change will be variations in your menstrual cycle due to hormone imbalance.

Menopause happens as the result of either natural processes or surgical procedures. Naturally, when a woman is of a certain age her ovaries release fewer hormones. Similarly, when your reproductive organs are surgically removed or blood supply is compromised, you will experience symptoms from the lack of hormones these missing organs once produced. Common symptoms of menopause include fatigue, depression, anxiety, cravings, mood swings, hot flashes and weight gain. It almost sounds like pregnancy! Before a women reaches menopause and her menstrual cycle completely ceases, she may experience symptoms for months or even years. As a teenager I can remember nearly suffering from frostbite in my grandmother's house, all because she was going through "the change." These

North Pole conditions went on for years. I also remember wondering what was taking "this change" so darn long. This perimenopause change before "the change" can be vexing to even the most cool and calm of women, but it is still nothing you cannot handle.

Every symptom has a solution. Crank up the air conditioning and turn on the fans when those personal summers I call hot flashes ignite your skin. Weight maintenance is a woman's cross to bear in and out of menopause. Yes, your fluctuating hormones will definitely add more of a challenge to weight loss, but it is far from impossible. Depression, anxiety, fatigue, and loss of libido can all be remedied with ramping up your sexual motor. Sex is a proven mood stabilizer and combats depression. I declare menopause is the time to bring sexy back.

Get Wet!

I am not menopausal, but I am not immune to the changes of life. In my twenties, I can recall just the thought of any particular six-foot tall, dark and handsome triggering a need to change my underwear. Now in my thirties, I find it takes a little more thought and time to get me gushing. Lessening and slowing of natural lubrication results from more than just age, but also certain medications and medical conditions can also affect your ability to get wet. Little known but common causes of vaginal dryness include tampon use, stress, exercise, diabetes and cancer.

Estrogen is one hormone with many responsibilities. Pertinently, it is responsible for the elasticity and moisture balance of the cells in your vaginal lining. With decreases of estrogen levels in menopause, women often complain of vaginal dryness and less stretch in the vaginal vault. Pliability aids the body to accommodate sexual activity. This lost estrogen can be replaced with topical creams, hormone-secreting rings, pellets or tablets. Also, I would like to inform you of the non-hormone options to increase vaginal readiness for intercourse. Moisturizing and lubricating are two important practices that we all need to consider adding to our regimen.

Most people are familiar with lubricants. These topical fluids are commonly applied to the vulva and vaginal areas to decrease friction. You should apply just prior to intercourse or masturbation to aid in the slip and slide of things that go bump in the night. These products are not just for intercourse with a partner, but feel free to use them during personal playtime as well. Lubricants can be applied to body parts, sex toys, vibrators and stimulators. You want to make sure they are safe for whatever form of play you may choose. Also beware of their interactions with contraception and condoms. It is important to educate yourself on all the different types and brands of personal lubricants. These fluids may be water-based, silicone-based, oil-based, or hybrids.

Water-based lubricants are the most common and generally the most latex-friendly. This attribute means it is the least likely to compromise the integrity of latex toys and condoms. The downside to this particular lube is due to the high water content. They are easily washed away in the water environments, which means they would not be optimal for sexy time in places like the shower or pool.

Silicone-based lubricants replace the water content with silicon. Therefore, you can feel free to use them for water play. Also, lubes with silicone tend to have a longer lasting silkiness than those that are water-based. Most of these liquids are also latex safe, but carefully read the label to be sure. Unfortunately, these fluids are not safe for silicone sex toys. Silicone-based lubricants have been shown to breakdown the rubber and silicone materials used to make sex toys, vibrators and stimulators.

Oil-based lubricants, as signified by the name, are constituted with oils. These lubes last even longer than their silicone-based counterparts. You can also apply them all over the body for a sensual massage. A very important thing to note, the oil in these products are not safe for latex condoms. Also their residue may be difficult to clean up. The oils stick to sex toys and may stain fabrics. Newer commercially sold lubricants may be hybrids. These fluids are more complex solutions to offer the natural feel of water but last longer similar to silicon and oil.

Moisturizers, like lubricants, combat vaginal dryness. Vulvar and vaginal moisturizing should be a regular, in some cases daily, practice. Once absorbed into the skin, moisturizers plump and replenish the cellular lining of these intimate areas to provide a natural moisture barrier that lasts longer than lubricants alone. Popular commercial brands of vaginal lubricants often also offer vaginal moisturizers. These solutions often contain glycerin, mineral oil and synthetic emollients. These products may also have preservatives and additives.

Natural oils are a suitable alternative to commercial products to provide regular moisture to the vulva, vagina and entire body. Similar to lubricants, please remember that oils may degrade latex and cause condoms to tear. Sweet almond, coconut, jojoba, olive, and flaxseed oil are acceptable for inmate moisturizing. The natural fatty acid, antioxidant, and antimicrobial activities make them ideal for nourishing and protecting your sensual areas.

Lubricants and moisturizers are not only for women in the affairs of menopause. Any woman looking to add silkiness and decrease friction should consider these products. Yes, moisturizers and lubricants can be used simultaneously. However women looking to conceive should note that some of these solutions might impair sperm motility and viability. Also, women not looking to conceive should be aware that any products containing oil can cause condoms, diaphragms, and dental dams to rip or tear. You never want to sacrifice safety. Make sure the product is hypoallergenic and safe for sensitive skin. Whichever type or brand you choose, it would greatly behoove you to always read the entire label in order to decide what product will work best for you.

Moisturize versus Lubricate

Moisturize
- Daily
- Replenish and Protect
- Natural Oils or Commercial products

Lubricate
- Sexual Activity
- Decreases friction
- Water- Silicone- Oil-based or Hybrid

Don't Let Gravity Get You Down

My main adversary in my battle with aging is gravity. I notice my skin sags and my eyelids droop. The downward pull on your pelvic floor can cause leaky bladders and prolapsed vaginas. You have to fight gravity. Nourish the collagen in your skin to promote elasticity. Do your Kegels and pelvic floor exercises to strengthen your core and lift the contents of your pelvis.

I am more of an advocate for clean eating and an active lifestyle than I am for drug therapy. There are several foods, plants, and herbs that support hormone production. Reestablishing hormone balance with natural remedies can relieve some of the symptoms of menopause. Plant soy and Black Cohosh are all natural alternatives for hot flashes and anxiety. Exercise, yoga, dancing, and of course sex are cardiovascular activities that promote good heart health and are natural antidepressants. Resistance training builds muscle and reduces the excess fat that has been known to increase hormonal imbalance.

Menopause comes with age and it seems no one wants to get older. I personally do not mind getting older, because I am not quite ready for the alternative to aging. If you are not getting older, then you are more than likely dead. My only desire is to age gracefully. I do not allow myself to get down and depressed with the constant ticking of time. Instead, I live my life by seconds and the minutes to cherish every moment. My age has brought me life experiences and maturity that I would not trade for anything. Don't get down – get up…and fight!

Enjoy the Ride!

I thoroughly enjoy asking women to relay the attributes of Menopause that bring them pleasure, and their responses give me great hope. Some women report that menopause has made them smarter. They feel as if the transition has taught them a lot about their bodies and their health. Other women report a sense of freedom. They are free from some of life's uncertainty. No more worries of menstrual periods and fear of unexpected pregnancies. One wise lady told me she was free from the average person's perception of what defines womanhood. She felt as if she had lived in her skin long enough to know exactly who she was and wanted to be. Her womanhood was not defined by the ability to reproduce, but the ability to live as a sexual being. Many women report improvement in their sex drive and sexual experience after menopause. Menopause took away any leftover excuses to not get your freak on.

Society and media would have you believe that sex is only for the young of age, but I am a firm believer that sex will keep you young at heart. In menopause, women can easily lose a sense of femininity and vitality because a part of their being is perceived as dead. However, if you asked a gardener, the prettiest rose needs regular pruning to blossom with beauty. Menopause is no more than a little pruning of your sexual flower.

I told you, I am looking forward to menopause and retirement. I may be on a fixed income, but I am making provisions right now for a convertible of some sort and multiple vacations in my golden years. I am also budgeting for all the moisturizers, lubricants and great sex in my future as well. Perception is reality. I perceive menopause as yet another phase of transition in womanhood, evolution. My future reality is not a wrinkled old lady, but my creases are the petals of mature and blossoming flower.

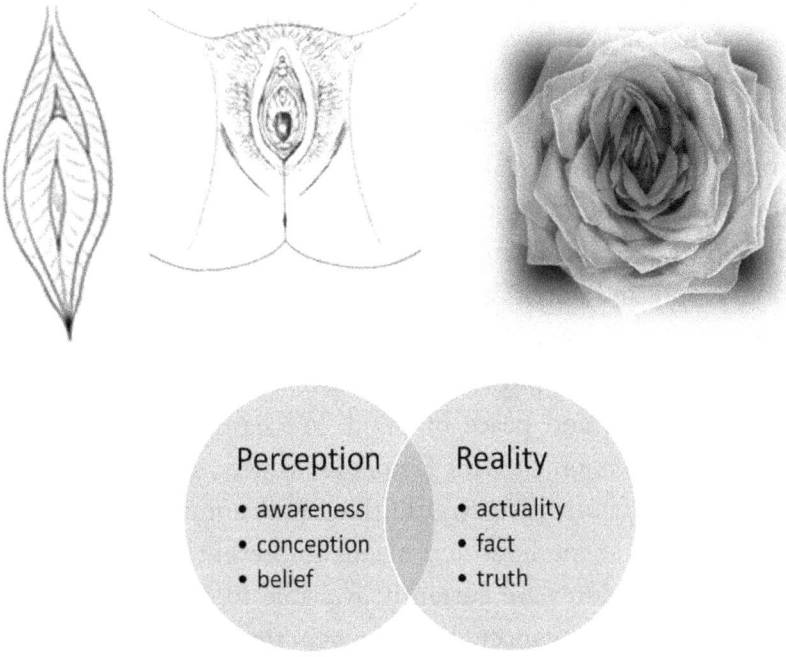

SEX AFTER...

CHAPTER 10: ...CANCER

If there is one diagnosis no person ever wants to hear, I think I would have to be cancer. Cancer is a leading cause of death amongst all members of the human race. Regardless of race, sex or religion, you have more than likely been affected by this horrible disease. Whether you are a fighter, survivor or supporter, you know the havoc it wreaks on the lives of patients and their families. Cancer is an abnormal overgrowth of cells that can happen in just about any organ system in the body. The abnormal cells grow very rapidly and literally rob the normal cells of their blood supply and nutrition. For that very reason and many more, I call cancer the worst kind of thief, the Great Thief. Cancer will attempt to steal your physical health and strength, as well as your mental fortitude and peace of mind. We have an obligation to educate ourselves on the risk factors for cancer, such as smoking cigarettes and family history. Additionally, you must make it your business to know methods and means to prevent cancer. Regular screening procedures are currently available to detect pre-cancer and early signs of cancer. Regular pap smears can detect the presence of abnormal cells in the female reproductive system. There are colonoscopy screenings for cancers in your colon and rectum. As a physician I can never abandon my oath to promote good health. I want everyone who reads this book to be armed with the knowledge to prevent an encounter with the Great Thief. However, if you or anyone you love has to fight the fight, I want to arm you with the power to give cancer hell.

Take it Easy, but Keep it Moving

Never forget to breathe. When you need to focus, or just gather your running emotions, take a slow methodical inhale and exhale. If you can breathe, you can live. If you are going to fight for your life you need a good game plan, a strong will, and ice cream. Your plan must have an offense and a defense, and defense wins championships. Your defense is all about containing the cancer and stopping its progression. Research and treatment protocols have made many advances. As a physician, I definitely recommend a multi-modal approach. Your team should consist of doctors and healthcare professional to direct your medical management. A nutritionist can structure your diet to optimize your main energy sources that nourish and protect your healthy cells and organs. Therapists, counselors, family and friends can form a necessary support system to nurture your mental fortitude. Some of the roughest, strongest skirmishes are fought on the battlefields of our consciousness. Positivity begets positivity. Think positive, live positive and rest positive.

Offensive strategies are all about gains. You want to get and keep the upper hand when it comes to the Great Thief, and sex is my secret weapon. I am very aware how crazy my last statement will seem to many. I only ask that you hear me out. Anecdotally, I have noticed over the years that patients with cancer diagnoses that continue to report sexual activity report less pain, less depression ad more consistent hopefulness for recovery. Remember, the Great Thief's mission is to steal your sense of normalcy, so your best efforts to maintain your regular routines and lifestyle area the best method to combat these attempts to derail you. Do not be overwhelmed with the tedious tasks of day-to-day life, but instead make it a point to enjoy as many of the activities you enjoyed before your diagnosis, including sex. You may need to make modifications to your routine but the goal is simply enjoyment.

Recalling one of my grandmother's adages, I can hear her saying, "Don't let the devil steal your joy." I say, "Don't let cancer steal your mojo." During treatment and recovery, you should acknowledge your sexuality and redefine your sex. Not all sex requires penetration. Intercourse is all about the interaction and sensual touch. The touch of the human hand has been proven to possess healing powers. So make time to get skin-to-skin. Whether you are spending quality time all by your lonesome or engaging a special someone, you should remain in the driver's seat and set the pace. Move with your personal level of comfort, but just keep moving. Envision your destination of remission and incarceration of the Great Thief. I know and believe it to always be possible to fight the winning fight, even until death.

Healing Hurts

When anyone receives a cancer diagnosis, in order to rebuke the thoughts of a death sentence, we tunnel vision on survival and forget to actually *live*. What's the difference? Similar to thinking, believing and knowing, a cancer patient is not exactly sure what to think or believe. The only thing they surely know is that they have a disease. Sadly, few know what cancer really means. I charge all healthcare professionals to do their best to educate these patients and help them understand their prognosis beyond statistics and Internet searches. When your day-to-day agenda revolves around doctor's appointments and drug regimens, you may allow yourself to go numb and not engage with the world around you. Intense counseling and preparation should be implemented prior to treatment. Knowledge gives our patients the power to hope and mentally fortifies a weakening body with faith in the medicines and treatment plan. On the other hand, a survivor knows they have a disease, but they also know they will live on if they have the will to fight with every single breath. Slow and steady wins the race. If you can inhale and exhale, you are still living. So as long as you are living, you are winning and healing. From day one, promise yourself you will not forget to live. You will remember to speak life. You will tell your loved ones around you that you love them. You will also share when you are scared and allow them to comfort you and reinforce your assurance that together you will all victoriously beat cancer. You will trust a higher power. You will remember to watch sunsets, laugh, and live. You do not have to wait until remission or the cure to be a survivor. Every day you live beyond that day of your diagnosis you are not just surviving you are living the life you were meant to live with love and the audacity to defy any predicted odds.

I never say it will be easy, but I always say it is possible. Treatment for cancer can sometimes feel just as harsh as the diagnosis. Surgery may be required to physically cut and remove the pathology from your body. Chemotherapeutic medications and radiations are used to target the abnormal cancer cells, but also indiscriminately take a toll on your mental and physical health as well. It appears to tear you down to your bare bones, but I want you to know those bones are a strong foundation you can use to rebuild.

Teach Me How to Kegel

This activity is not a new dance craze. A Kegel is a self-induced contraction of the musculature that comprises your pelvic floor. Your pelvis houses the majority of your reproductive organs. Think of your pelvic floor as a shelf or mantle holding these prized possessions. The simplest way to identify this group of muscles is to attempt to stop your stream while urinating. The muscles you engage to stop the flow of urine make up the stabilizing infrastructure of your pelvis. This method is only used to identify the muscle group – do not make regular practice of stopping your flow of urine! This repeated action can prevent your bladder from emptying and increase your risk for urinary tract infections (UTI). You can also physically feel these muscles contracting by placing two fingers in your vaginal vault and attempting to clench your sex around your digits.

Now that you have distinguished these coveted muscles, you should practice contracting them throughout the day. Repeated tightening builds strength and support. Every woman should add three or four sets of Kegels to their daily routine. Consider doing them during the commercials of your favorite television show. If you really want a challenge you can also use vaginal weights, Ben Wa balls, or Burmese bells for additional resistance. The more you exercise your sexual core will result in more blood flow to these sensitive areas. Improved circulation can in turn enhance your arousal and stimulation.

Kegels can be physically and mentally therapeutic. Your breathing pattern should be in sync with your contractions. Inhale as your contract and exhale as you release. Your pace should be slow and steady. Repetition can actually lull you into a sereneintrospection. Your thoughts should be focused on positivity. Imagine all the shattered pieces of your brokenness placed back in rightful order one by one. Meditate on healing, love, and light. Each contraction is strengthening your sacred core, and each breath allow you to harness the mental fortitude to conquer anything standing in the way of what is rightfully yours – the right to life.

Sex is Good Medicine

I believe with all of my heart that sex is the superlative antidote. The benefits of regular sexual activity are endless, from improved cognition to even prolonging life. Sex is truly an ally in cancer and disease prevention. If you do not believe me, do your own research. Scientific journals, reputable research facilities, doctors and scientists alike publish paper after paper to document the proven benefits of masturbation, intercourse, and orgasms. Sex is good medicine.

Sex heals and should not hurt.Nevertheless, the disease process of cancer, as well as medicines and procedures designed for its treatment, can have debilitating side effects. For example, vaginal dryness can cause discomfort during intercourse. Also, surgical wounds, scar tissue, and muscle spasms can cause sex to be unpleasant. Uncomfortable sex is unacceptable. The one mandatory requirement for sex is that it must be pleasurable. If it is not pleasurable, it is not sex. So if you ever experience pain, you should seek out your healthcare professional for consultation. The remedy could be as simple as adding moisturizers and lubricants to your regimen. For more complicated pelvic floor dysfunction, physical therapy specialists can guide your rehabilitation. One must also consider that maybe the stress and emotional toll can have physical manifestations. It never hurts to regularly take a self-evaluation of your mental wellbeing. When you need insight and guidance, there are trained counselors and therapists willing to help. Again, a team approach to comprehensive healthcare is always optimal.

At no point from diagnosis to treatment and even in remission should you have to sacrifice your sexuality on the altar of disease and sickness. This sacred sense of self should be unapologetically showcased no matter what trials and tribulations you endure. Do not let cancer tear down your personal image because of the toll it may take on your physical appearance. Cancer may have altered your anatomy, but cancer will never touch your inner beauty and strength. If you have concerns and anxiety about restarting a sexual relationship, you have to be able to communicate those reservations with your partner. If you do not feel comfortable talking about your feelings, you should not feel comfortable sharing your vagina either. Do not burden yourself with the pressure of pleasing your mate right away. Take care of yourself first. Find your G-spot again. Put on your best vixen wig and satin lingerie even if it is for your eyes only. Rekindle your fire!

SEX AFTER...

CHAPTER 11: ...DRUGS

I embrace my life of irony. I find humor in the fact that I am an Anesthesiologist charged with medically inducing thousands of patients into a state a sleep, yet I have been terribly unsuccessful in getting my toddler to sleep through the night. I am a physician that prescribes and administers medicine. However, I struggle to take my vitamins and refuse to take prescribed medications on a regular basis. As a healthcare professional, I am committed to preventive maintenance, nutrition, fitness, mental fortitude and safe sex. I am just not a fan of pills. I really believe that most people need to exercise, eat healthy, and have more sex instead of taking multiple medications every day. Still, I have come to the realization that if anyone lives long enough in this age of managed healthcare, one of my colleagues is bound to find an ailment worthy of a prescription. It seems that if you live in Louisiana with its excellent Creole and Cajun cuisine, high blood pressure and cholesterol are bound to be a part of your medical history or future. But no worries, we have a couple of pills for what ails you. Not me! I will modify my diet and run like someone I owe money is chasing me before I resolve to digest capsules of foreign man-made material every day for the rest of my life.

Modern medicine and all of its advances continue to stamp out diseases, many of which were at one time thought to be inevitably fatal. Yet for all the good medicine does, one should never turn a blind eye to the many side effects. We take pills for everything. We have pills to help us concentrate and keep our minds from wandering. This same medicine makes the heart race and elevates blood pressure. We take pills to stay awake and then we need pills to go to sleep. How does one keep track of what pill does what, when, and how? I am struggling to eat my recommended fruits and vegetables. I have no desire to depend on a daily pill regimen to sustain my vigor and wellbeing.

Know Your Side Effects

Whenever I begin counseling my patients about smoking cessation, I try to take a different approach. I do not talk about tobacco abuse and increased risk for cancer. I point out the fact that smoking causes wrinkles and other deformities that really grab the attention of a vain individual. I do not believe all of my patients are that self-absorbed, but I like to see the surprised look on their face when I am not confronting them with the normal rhetoric. With all the recent publicity and anti-smoking campaigns, the average adult knows that smoking causes cancer, yet they continue to light up. However, I doubt these women have thought about combating deeper, more pronounced smile lines and loss of lip volume. Especially in this day and age, it seems like plump kissable lips are in the highest of demand. Once I have their attention, I try to offer nicotine alternatives not to replace the cigarette but to decrease cravings with the ultimate goal of completely quitting.

Many commonly used medications to treat high blood pressure, depression, and pain also commonly share sexual dysfunction as a known side effect. Sexual dysfunction defines any abnormality or deficiency in the normal sexual cycle from libido to arousal and climax. Antidepressants may decrease your sexual drive and desire. These drugs may also interfere with your ability to achieve an orgasm. I am depressed just thinking about an inability to climax. Many adults are willing to accept the need to take pills every day for the rest of their life. I should hope that just as many adults would consider adopting healthier diets and getting active with a regular exercise regime to achieve lower blood pressure without sexual side effects.

As an even better alternative, regular sexual activity decreases blood pressure prevents high blood pressure. I am by no means saying that medication is completely unnecessary. I am promoting sexual activity to allow your body to heal itself and possibly decrease the need for medications. What is the harm is trying? What could be so bad about trying to lower your stress level and augment your mood with more sex? Sex decreases your risk for certain cancers, heart disease, depression, and other mental health ailments. Sex is great medicine.

Physicians Practice Medicine, but You Live Life

I am a doctor, but more specifically I am an Anesthesiologist. I provide epidurals and other techniques to manage the pain associate with child birth. I also administer medications for patients having surgery to induce sleep and manage pain. I tell people all the time how I chose my specialty. During my matriculation at Howard University, I decided early on I wanted a career that did not involve a clinic. I did not want to have a medical office where people would stop in to regularly complain about all that was going wrong with their lives without any accountability. Or even worse, you have some patients that never complain and you never find out anything is wrong until they end up in the emergency room on the brink of death. I am a woman of action. When I decided on a career in healthcare, I wanted to take an active role in ridding the world of sickness and disease. As soon as I stepped foot in the operating room of Howard University Hospital, I felt I had found my true calling. The operating room is the place where surgeons remove the cancer. They cut out the infection. This place is also where trauma is repaired. Gunshot holes, stab wounds and broken bones are mended so healing can begin. Everyone is actively involved in truly eradicating disease. No one is standing around handing out prescriptions.

All the same, when I decided to add sexuality counseling to my practice, I did not want to manufacture a clinic for sexual dysfunction. My office is not the place where people should expect to come and complain about all that is lacking in their sex life. Every lecture, office visit, seminar, and book has and will be about a very personal journey each and every individual takes to discover, accept and embrace one of their most powerful assets. Counseling should be professionally assisted personal enlightenment. As a professional I use my learned skillset to assist you, the person, on a journey of self-discovery. My goal is to provide a safe environment to unearth both strengths and weaknesses. Furthermore, I hope to provide you with the tools to compensate for those weaknesses and heal whatever is broken. No one leaves my counseling practice with prescriptions, but every client leaves with homework. My whole agenda is about empowering an individual to do their work and find wholeness from brokenness.

I may be a doctor, but I also have my own diverse team of healthcare providers. I have an Internal Medicine Physician, an Obstetrician/Gynecologist, a nutritionist, a chiropractor, a physical therapist, a Psychiatrist, a therapist, and a dentist. I am serious about my health, and not just some of my health but *all* of my health. Anytime I have a lab test done, I share the results with my entire team. Anytime I have a new symptom, such as fatigue or pain, I am going to share this information with the team and look for feedback. Please believe that all of my team members know they should always be ready to present a solution that does not involve taking a pill. I have used herbs, essential oils, and strengthening exercises to combat my own health issues. There have been times where I could not avoid taking prescribed medicines. Before the prescription can be filled, I have to know the dose, side effects, and expected duration of the medicine. For me a pill will always be the last resort. Did I mention doctors make the worst patients?

I hope my colleagues do not begrudge my next few statements. Your physician works for *you*. All of your healthcare providers are enlisted members on your team to serve you and your health interests. In return, you, the patient, must never equate their years of education and training to your most recent Internet search. A responsible patient should be actively involved in their healthcare experience. I want patients to keep track of their appointments and preventive screenings. Every patient is well within their rights to seek out multiple opinions from separate medical disciplines. I have referred my patients to physical therapist and chiropractors for a multi modal approach to chronic pain. I have also enlisted the help of pelvic floor physical therapists and specialized trauma therapists to provide the best care for my post trauma clientele. The best doctor is not the one who never needs help, but the one who knows when to ask for help.

Think about your last doctor's visit. What did you and your healthcare provider discuss? Were you forthcoming with any new symptoms? Did you review any medicines you are taking? Do you know what medicines you are taking and why you are taking them? Is the dose or amount of medicine you are taking effective? Do your doses need to be adjusted? Have you ever discussed other alternative healthcare practices? Questions need answers and you owe it to yourself to know your body and all of its ailments in order to establish a plan of care. You are just as accountable for your state of health as your doctors, nurses and therapists. You all should be working together for the most beneficial outcome. Pills and medicines treat existing diseases and conditions. Vaccinations have come a long way in preventing and nearly eradicating some illnesses. Call me old fashioned, but I still think both pale in comparison to clean living, proper nutrition and regular exercise, including sexual activity.

SEX AFTER...

CHAPTER 12: ...SALVATION

Every human being is fearfully and wonderfully made with a default reaction to change. New things, experiences, and people trigger fear andangst. I need everyone to take a moment and download a new operating system called *love*. It is the easiest thing to love the familiar. I am asking you love the foreign. Embrace something new. First, you will have to abandon these longstanding notions of shame and antipathy previously associated with sexuality. I need you to know that being sex-positive does not equate to sexually promiscuous or any kind of deviant behavior. All it means is that you accept the power of love, the power to be loved and let love.

I am often questioned about my motives to empower women to embrace their sexuality while simultaneously proclaiming to be very spiritual. I find spirituality and sexuality to be two sides of the same coin. We humans are sexual and spiritual beings. We are divinely made in a physical form that our hands can touch, and also a transcending essence that our hearts can feel. With ease the average person accepts the fact that a body without a heart, brain, breath and blood flow is incompatible with life. But we seem to forget that without sex, all life ceases to exist. Every child is born through the loins of woman. Aside from Immaculate Conception, birth is preceded by sex. So my sexuality has been part my existence from birth. As I see it, my spiritual self makes me a descendent of divinity. My spirit connects me to my beliefs and my faith in a higher power. Just the same, my sexuality makes me magical. My sexual self, when nourished, transcends the natural and can only be described as supernatural. Envision the exquisite communication of bodies touching and spirits dancing. In my mind's eye that is how I see sex. Sex organs intertwined in a staccato dance. Hearts and minds consumed in an unparalleled exchange. One could call it magical.

Love Trumps Hate Every Time

I have no desire to argue the validity of religious preference or doctrine. Frankly, if any sect or creed is not founded on the basis of loving one another as a human race, their ideology is flawed beyond repair and just not worth the effort. I come with a message of love, kindness, and a never-ending pursuit of happiness. I do believe these principles are inalienable rights. I want you to love your fellow man just as you love yourself.

Matter of fact, I want you do be an expert at loving yourself, because I believe that is how loving others becomes second nature. I had to learn early in my career that a sick doctor heals few, if any, patients. As you can imagine, most patients will not have a great deal of confidence in a doctor who appears to be in poor health. I make it a priority to take care of my physical, mental and sexual health in order to be the best physician I can be. I love me in the best way I know how to love a human being.

Therefore, I am more than capable of loving others, and I can also recognize when others are ill-equipped to love me.

Sex is Spiritual

Every human being has a heart. The heart is the motor, pumping nourishing blood throughout the body. The heart warms the physical being. Beyond these actions, the heart is thought to be the domicile of admiration and adoration. Thus, I believe you heart is indeed a sex organ. Sexuality encompasses more than the physical activity of having sex. Your sexuality is intertwined with the basic traits of humanity. Simply put, your sexuality is a large determinant of how you love. Human beings are designed to have feelings and emotions. Humans have an innate need to use our five God-given senses (seeing, hearing, smelling, touching and tasting). We all exist with the desire to discover and connect with the world around us. This curiosity defines the essence of our spirit being. Your coveted aspirations, whether hidden or made known, guide your thoughts and actions. Because I love with my whole being, I get to connect with the world around me in ways I had never imagined.

I lost my religion when I found salvation a long time ago. I found most ritualistic practices of religion put way too many restrictions on love. Call me a hopeful optimistic, but I want to believe we human beings of mind, body and spirit can and should thrive on love and not law. Let your moral compass guide your thoughts, words and deeds. I refused to be confined by customs and popular definitions of normalcy. I respect a higher power, consciousness, and a spirit of freedom. I embrace salvation and freedom. No one can tell me who or how to love. I am free to love whomever and however I choose. Now that's salvation!

Sex Saves!

Early in my career as a sexuality counselor, I was invited to speak to a group of women at a golf club in Flint, Michigan. This very intimidating audience consisted of known church-going women, my mother, and her older sister. The women's ages ranged from early twenties up to late seventies. Also, tucked away in the back room, my teenage cousin was babysitting my seven-month-old daughter. There I stood with several sets of eager eyes awaiting my opening words. I thought briefly that maybe I should sing a hymn or something. However, as I introduced myself and the topic of the discussion for the evening, I realized these women knew good and well what kind of seminar they had signed up for weeks prior to the event. They had driven in the blistering cold of Michigan winter weather to hear me talk about sex. So by the grace of God, I had to deliver!

I proceeded to encourage these women to embrace their sexual health. We discussed hygiene, masturbation, moisturizers and lubricants. Please do not forget, my mother and older aunt were sitting in the audience as I demonstrated finger foreplay while using my hand to mimic a vaginal vault. To my surprise, neither one of them sat with any looks of disgust. I saw some of these ladies taking notes. Thought provoking questions were being asked and answered. We as a group of sex-positive women were all engaged. We were having church.

Then one of the ladies asked a question that nearly broke my heart. She wanted to know what she could do if she thought it had just been too long, and her sexual time had passed. I wanted to encourage her and let her know that sexuality never dies. I needed her to understand that sexuality is a fluid and evolving part of every person's being. Sex is a part of being human. No matter how long it has been since your last sexual encounter, the next time is a new opportunity to start over. Start at the beginning – with discovery and self-pleasure. Many mature women are concerned with how to engage their mates after long periods of abstinence. Sex can be the dance of two souls. Just as you chose a partner, you can choose the song and dance. Sex can mean different things to different people as time changes. Some older couples are not always able to engage in the acrobatics of younger couples, but that is not what intercourse is really about. Sex is about pleasure. It's about whispered words of passion, seductive caresses and intimate kisses. Those are all sex. I repeat: Sexuality is fluid. It has to evolve with each individual's life. We all have to be willing to go with the flow of change and make necessary modifications to achieve intimacy. Never let fear block you from success. No one wants to be left with a life of regret. Therefore, giving up can never be an option.

A believer's salvation is rooted in faith, a belief in redemption. We believers are redeemed and delivered from the tempter's guiles and snares, so live free. Liberate your mind from self-imposed limitations. You are not too old. You need not be afraid. If the end has already been written and victory already proclaimed, why would you give up now? You have to press on, because I truly believe the best is yet to come. I have just enough faith to know that I am meant for something greater. My conviction will not let me surrender to a boring existence, and I pray that no one ever surrenders such a prize possession as their sexuality.

Let Me Testify!

I had the pleasure of growing up in what has been prophetically and affectionately labeled as the "Bible Belt" of this great country. Most of my family is affiliated with the Baptist sect. Growing up in church, I can recall my favorite part of the service was always devotion and testimony. The choir and musicians would get the congregation so fired up with the angelic singing. Those skilled musicians could have easily backed up any rhythm and blues headliner. My pastor had one of those melodious voices that would stir those church sisters to shouting and praising the most high just short of throwing their panties at the pulpit. Then the testimonies would begin. This is the part of service where any random individual could come and tell the congregation just how good God had been to them. I am telling you these people would proclaim the largest to the smallest victories, and all the same one overzealous believer after the other would jump off the celebratory dancing. I don't care if you were proclaiming cancer remission or a healed ingrown toenail, the saints were going into a worshipping frenzy.

Now do not get me wrong. I believe God is worthy of all the praise you have to offer, but here is my problem: I have yet to conjure a collaborative exaltation of the sexual beings that God created us all to be. We were created and endowed from birth with sex. We innately have sexual organs, sexual thoughts, and sexual activities. God is the creator of all beings, and he designed living things, human and animal, to be born from the sex organs of a woman. Furthermore as Christians, faith is founded on the belief that the savior was born of an untouched and sacred sex. So why can I not get these blood-bought believers to celebrate the magic that is sex? Why are women not respectedfor the vessels of life we are? Also in regards to our bodies as temples, our bodies are the composite of the physical (skin, bone muscle, organs), mind and spirit. Should we not take care to maintain these shrines of flesh and essence in the best of health? Does that not include sexual awareness and health?

I love God. I love humanity. And I love sex. I believe sex is a form of worship. Also, I believe in the Bible. I take to heart the scriptures of Solomon that depict brazened young ladies and elaborate descriptions of the cedar ceiling from the vantage point as she lies on her back engaging her lover in the most intimate of soul to soul dances. Yes the Bible speaks of sex, so the church needs to have a good "come to Jesus" conversation about it too. It is past time to get real.

Celebrity, Not Celibacy

I am often asked about my views on celibacy, but few really want to hear what I have to say. People need to understand what celibacy represents. Celibacy is a personal sacrifice. Celibacy is a personal choice that goes beyond just abstaining from sexual intercourse. It is also a vow to remain without a partner. Few people understand the difference between celibacy, abstinence and chasteness. So since I am already dropping knowledge, I need to also tell you what celibacy is not. Just because you find yourself in a situational drought without a partner to engage in sexual activity, you are not celibate. You may be desperate and lacking, but celibate you are not. Those circumstances would mirror my intent to tell others I am fasting just because I forgot my money to buy lunch. You are not honestly able to sacrifice something if you can't access it or possess it. To be celibate, you have to denounce the desire for companionship. Again, celibacy is a personal surrender of sexuality. I do not begrudge anyone the right to choose, just as I hope no one would harbor any resentment of my personal choices.

I chose celebrity and not celibacy. I chose to be a world-renowned superstar for self-pleasure. I celebrate my sexuality, because it is a part of my testimony. I proclaim my essence as a woman. I am made in the mirror image of my sovereign

Creator to be exceptional. I revere my body as a holy vessel. I try to abstain from unhealthy practices and harmful substances. I do not engage in risky behavior. I try to love my neighbors as I love myself. I think I am doing a pretty good job, because I first learned how to love me.

The Benediction

I do fondly reflect on my childhood participation in church services. I am the woman I am today because of the little girl whose parent brought her church every Sunday. I learned to play many musical instruments and sing praises to God. Church gave me faith to believe in the unseen. Also, church taught me discipline and discipleship. My parents always taught me you are not a Christian because you are inherently good. You do good deeds and work towards the promise because you are a Christian. Being Baptist, I will not lie. As much as I enjoyed the weekly celebration, it seemed as if the service would go on forever. I would anxiously await any sign ofthe ceremony coming to the close. Thankfully, sooner or later every Sunday, worship would end with a blessed benediction, which was music to my ears! The Latin breakdown of the word literally means, "well speak." The pastor would always be sure to end service with an invocation of blessing, divine words for thought and well-wishing as the congregation dispersed from the sanctuary.

So in parting, I leave you with a few thoughts of my own. We are all flawed humans, and we need to liberate ourselves from unsolicited judgments. Embrace your flaws with determination to be better. If you are busy with the work of personal improvement, it leaves little time to judge other people and their imperfections. Quit caring what other people think about you, because it is really none of your business. Focus on love. Love yourself so you will be capable of loving others. Love saved me. I would not exist, live, and breathe had it not been for love. My birth came as a byproduct of sex. Thus, I conclude sex is life. Sex is living. Now let the church say, Amen!

SEX AFTER...

CHAPTER 13: ...DEATH

This book exists for this chapter. All the insights on the following pages are my personal testimony. I want you to take away lessons of hope and resolution from my initially sorrowful journey. I have no idea if there is truly a proper way to grieve a lost loved one. I am sure I made quite a few mistakes during my period of mourning. Honestly, some days I still feel like I am mourning. However, I take a great deal of solace in my abundant memories of joy and happiness remembering a person I consider gone, but never forgotten.

Gone but Never Forgotten

After my father passed away, I moved back to my hometown of Shreveport, Louisiana to be near my mother and brother. I had lost one parent, so I clung to my mother and only sibling for dear life. These two were my life-line. I moved and bought a house. My mother was still living in my childhood home, but the thought of living in that home where she and my dad shared decades of memories was not conducive to healing. So my mom moved into my home. I need you to grasp all of these monumental turns of events that shaped my personal evolution into womanhood. I had just graduated from my den of hyper sexuality, better known as medical school. I am not sure if it was the tedious, exhausting examination and near worship of human anatomy and physiology that unearthed frequent, uncontrolled primal urges and mayhem. I really think my escapades in higher education will be another book or reality show. Either way, I had returned to the Bible Belt of the south to bury my father. I was angry and disappointed at the same time in the early stages of grief and way too distracted to really understand the totality of my mother moving into my residence. In that moment, I just knew I would not allow her to sink into the despair of unrelenting memories of her dead husband in my childhood home. I know this all sounds like the makings of a comedic gospel screenplay, but these scenes of my reality were turning at warp speed. Remember, I was back in the city where I was born and raised to commence my career as a young minority female physician where very few would regard me as medical doctor. I was affectionately known to most as Alfred and Nora's daughter, or better yet Andre's little sister. For the most part it was a warm welcome home, but let us not forget the haters. I was not so affectionately, and I might add erroneously, known to a few as that mean, bourgeois girl from high school. I was a complicated ball of emotions trying to figure out how I could be a good daughter and support my mother who had lost the love of her life. Also remember I had lost the strongest man I had even known, my problem-solver. At that time I could not comprehend how my dad had left me with this big mess of a life – a heartbroken mother, hellacious workplace, and wavering faith in God.

I stumbled. My anger was indiscriminate. I was mad at my father for dying. I was vexed with my mom for simply not being my dad. I was irritated at my job for its endless demands. I was furious with myself for somehow not seeing all of this coming. It pains me to admit one of my biggest regrets: I was mad at God because He allowed this devastation to take up residence in the life of his proclaimed child. He took my dad. Now for a moment, fast forward to the here and now. I still believe all of those things but with a different perspective. Yes, God took my dad, but I also know Alfred Hall III was ready to meet his creator. I am comforted with thoughts that my dad is at eternal peace. I miss him. I love him. I wanted him to see me graduate and meet his granddaughter. Every time anything good happens in my life, almost immediately I wish he were present. In a way, I know he is present. I still hear his voice and his laughter. I live to make him proud, and I now know I would not be this strong, independent and resilient if he had not died. I need you to know that this peace and resolve is the result of years of prayer, counseling, and journaling. By no means did I awaken with an instant epiphany the day after my father died.

You are Still Very Much Alive

I still find it difficult to remember such indescribable sadness. I felt like I was drowning in sorrow, but held on to a sliver of hope. My life was a chaotic mess, but I still had a life. I had to come to terms with the fact that my loved one was the only person that died. I was indeed still living. It took my brother to remind me of the woman my dad had raised me to be. My last name was and is Hall. Hall women were never built for mediocrity. We were built to overcome and thrive. I know my dad would have never wanted me, or my mom, to stop living. So we could never dishonor his memory by giving up. I am his legacy. My mother, my brother and I vowed to live remembering Alfred Hall III forever, but not ache to join his corpse in the cemetery. This promise translated into a corporate commitment to live better.

All of three of us began to focus on not just existing in the absence of Mr. Hall. Our focus became thriving in good physical, mental and financial health. Just like shedding our grieving garments, we abandoned our battered, deep-fried comfort foods for more nutritious diets. We worked towards becoming more physically active. We dedicated a great deal of time to establish a non-profit organization to honor my dad in more than just name. The Alfred Hall III Foundation disperses financial endowments to young people seeking higher education and other people pursuing entrepreneurship. My dad made sure my brother and I were able to become college-educated professionals. Mr. Hall pushed us to achieve the degrees he coveted for his own, as he should have, considering my scholastic achievements would not have been possible without my dad. I am sure my brother would also agree with my sentiment. The foundation's annual scholarship funds ensure more young adults are blessed with similar opportunities to achieve and succeed.

My mother, my brother and I focused our resources on writing new chapters in our lives. We were all busy trying to live better and run our newcorporation. We were on a mission with a new purpose. I am comforted to think of all the good that came from the sad and painful passing of my father. That hard-learned lesson is the most beneficial token of wisdom I can impart to any grieving soul. Make sure something good comes from all the bad. My tears of mourning afforded me the opportunity to bring smiles to aspiring college students and their families.

Welcome to a New Normal

Back to adjusting to life without the man of the house. Dad was gone. Mom was living in my home. I was just about to work myself to death. I was in the hamster wheel of working and sleeping. I was unraveling and I started to notice my mom becoming withdrawn. I had to do something to de-stress and get my mom reengaged. So I decided to resurrect my dating life and I encouraged my mom to reach out to some of her best girlfriends.

One evening after returning from a disastrous date I found my mom on the sofa, conversing with a friend who was going through divorce. I began to recount the comedic elements of my evening with Mr. Wrong. Laughing was the best medicine. I just knew if I could find a way to get my friends together with my mom and her friends more laugher would ensue. So I went about the business of uniting a group of seemingly polar-opposite women. On one hand, you had my group of single, dating, newlywed, and/or new to motherhood lady friends. Then on the other, you had my mother and her post-menopausal, divorced, empty nesters and/or widowed lady friends. I was nearly salivating at the thought of the possibility for comic relief from such a sobering reality, but I reaped so much more. This group of diverse women set the scene for an empowering exchange. We shared food, wine, advice, heartache, and most importantly healing testimonies. Also, I was not disappointed with the entertainment factor. I laughed until I cried with these women. Then I realized laughter is good medicine.

In my new normal, I had to accept that things would never be the way they were, but there were still good times to be had by all. Also, I have to admit I needed my sisterhood to heal. I needed to share my pain and find a way to smile while waiting on that rainbow to eclipse the sky. I spent a great deal of time being strong for my mother, but she was the woman who raised me to be strong. She was no shrinking violet. We were both women warriors. Knowing my strength and realizing her strength restored my confidence that we could and would get through anything. We were hurting, but we were definitely healing.

Heal Your Way

I remember in the days after my dad's passing, countless friends and relatives brought casseroles and boxes of friend chicken. I truly lost count of all the birds that died in memory of Alfred Hall III. A few people offered to come clean the house. When it came time to move my mom into my house, I had no need for a moving company. Family, friends, church members, and pretty much the whole community helped us move. Everyone just wanted to help. They were there to do whatever was needed to help us heal from the grief. My faith in humanity was more than restored. In the midst of all that sadness, my heart was warmed by all of the generosity and sincere concern for the wellbeing of me and my family. I am still grateful to all those who stood in the gap, but still the burden to heal rested on our individual shoulders.

Luckily, I did not have to battle my grief and depression alone. My brother and mother were strong emotional supports. My brother and I would talk ad nauseam about our shared memories of life with my dad. We would laugh until we cried at our secret childhood hijinks. Some of those secrets I will take to the grave, but the laughter these memories evoked saved my life. Also, I found solace in my new role as life coach to my mother. I loved teaching my mother everything I knew about being a single, independent woman. I must admit the road was rough, but enjoyed the struggle. I also admit I take an unconventional delight in making my mom uncomfortable. It was so difficult to suppress my laughter and keep a straight face during our first "sex talk." My mom was so visibly uncomfortable with the topic of conversation, but I thought it was hilarious. She quickly became exasperated with all my talk of condoms, lubrication, and masturbation. My mom felt my tutelage was of no use to her, because she had no desire to be intimate with another man.

I am not a sick and twisted individual. I am very healthy, and I embrace my every curve. I never wanted to torture my mother. I just refused to let her sexuality die with my dad. So I did what any good sexuality counselor would do under these circumstances. I bought my dear mother her first vibrator and clitoris stimulator. I also disappeared for the weekend so the two could get acquainted.

Live On

I sincerely pray that someone approaches my husband at my funeral to inquire how I passed away to eternal rest and he can honestly respond, "On top of me!" I want to live my life up until I take my very last breath. In a roundabout way, the death of so many people I have loved over my lifetime has given purpose to my life. My maternal aunts died during my adolescence. These women were some characters. My Aunt Leola told me at the age of around seven or eight that one day I would realize the power entrusted in between my legs if was as smart as she believed me to be. My dear Auntie, I am one smart cookie. I found my voice, and I know I am loud. My paternal grandfather, Alfred Hall II, told me to speak up because the world needed to hear what I had to say.

My dear dad, Alfred Hall III, raised me like his princess. He loved me unconditionally. He constantly bragged to his family, friends and coworkers about his children. If you would have listened to him speak of my brother and me, you might think we were fictional characters or comic book heroes. Still, Mr. Hall will forever be my real life hero. I live every day of my life as an affirmation of his legacy. I work hard just like he taught me by example. My love of family mirrors his sentiment.

I know there is no way my dad would have left his family unless he was confident we would thrive. In hindsight, I believe he recognized my potential before I did. He knew my brother was the man he had raised him to be. He had witnessed my mother's unshakeable faith to hold her family together. I sure miss watching sports with my dad. We were both avid fans. He would always stress to me the advantage of the team with the best players who knew how to play their positions. I believe my dad had to transition into playing his best position as guardian angel to his beloved family.

I need you take a few things way from my journey. First, life does indeed go on, so please live it. I want you to find a way to smile through the tears. Also, you need to lean on somebody. You can always depend on yourself, but every so often let a like-hearted soul inspire your greatness. I am so thankful for every strong woman whose iron sharpened my iron. I am blessed to have been raised by a strong man who was strong enough to let his queen and princess shine.

SEX AFTER...

CHAPTER 14: ...EMPOWERMENT

The pursuit of pleasure is your undeniable birthright. I want you to feel entitled. I have poured my heart and soul into these pages, unearthed my flaws and insecurities to bare my soul. I want you to get just as naked, and then clothe yourself in garments of confidence and sensuality. I want you to see yourself as a sexual being. I want you to acknowledge your primitive desires and seek out kindling for the sultry fire that stirs your soul. I want your toes to curl, heart to race, and temperature to rise. I want the wait to be over. I want you to realize that permission has been sought and granted. You bought this book, so put it into practice. You are liberated from the constraints of your own mind. I dare you to dream big.

Dreams are visions that most dare not attempt to accomplish. Your dreams are not unreachable like the stars. All you desire from your sex is well within your reach, so grab it. Clutch what you once thought to be unattainable. Masterfully masturbate until you climax. Embrace your partner in the spirit of spontaneity. Find their erotic zones. Tempt, tease and stimulate their pleasure points until you bring them to the brink of insane bliss. Put in that work, then bask in the afterglow.

Bask in the Afterglow

Afterglow is the term many use to describe the lingering state of fulfilled satisfaction after an orgasm. In all actuality, afterglow is defined as the persisting illumination even after the light source has disappeared. For example, the evening sky will have an afterglow well after the sun has set. After my lectures are done and this book is read, I hope you never forget all that you have learned. I hope your personal quest for more knowledge of self and sex is not a dimly lit one, but a blazing path of fiery hot orgasm.

Getting started on the road to sexual promise is scary because you are not sure of all the obstacles that may stand in your way. Attempting to restart and reclaim your sexual identity is just as frightening, because you may be very aware of the frustrations and failures awaiting your footsteps like landmines. We already know the first time was disappointing for most, so think of it as room for improvement. No matter if it is your first time or starting over, I want you to be confident that you can enjoy sex. You can enjoy sex by yourself or with a partner of your choosing. You have no need to fear the unknown. Uncover it! Find all those hidden hot spots. Discover your deepest desires and fantasies, then recreate each lustful scene. I hope you realize and accept that you deserve everything good that comes your way. Bask in the afterglow of victory.

Do not Fake it Until you Make it

Have you ever faked an orgasm? My concern is not with the falsehood. I really want to address the reasons why women feel the need to fake climaxing. Most commonly, women feign climax because they are engaged in sexual activity that is not pleasurable. Thus they just want the uncomfortable ordeal to be over. Sadly, other women simulate true arousal because they were never stimulated to begin with and are unable to reach a true climax. Women have been poorly conditioned to believe sex is really for the man and not the woman. That disgusting rhetoric has further brainwashed women to feel responsible for their partner's satisfaction and neglect their own. So then we women folk moan, groan, and coo to bolster a man's ego and allow them to believe there are superior lovers. In reality, you are doing not only yourself but your other sisters in womanhood a disservice. That unjustly inflated ego will leave one woman's bed and land in another one armed with your false cries of ecstasy instead of the truth. I am not saying it is your job to tear the man down for the piss poor lover you know him to be. I only want you to be honest and prevent that man from disappointing another lover.

I never want you to feel the need to fake an orgasm again. I want you to experience true unadulterated pleasure at your own hand. When you are knowledgeable about all the areas of your body that crave stimulation, you can simply direct your partner down lover's lane to climax cove. A well-learned student can make the best teacher. Learn your pleasure points. Know what you need to get to that highest peak of sensual stimulation, then guide your partner to recreate that sweet bliss for both of you.

Please Use Your Powers for Good, Not Evil

I hope this book starts a never-ending conversation among the newly empowered and soon to be sexually liberated. I did not begin this journey to fail. I never dream with the intention for my vision to eternally rest in the crevices of my imagination. Just as I instructed you in previous chapters, I now have taken pen to paper and drafted the imaginary into concrete imagery to share with all of womanhood. My mission to save the world one orgasm at a time starts with my challenge to masterfully masturbate to satiety. Once you accept the mission, dare to not stop. Reach another soul by teaching another soul. Just as you and girlfriends gather to gossip and sip tea, I want the topics of sexual health and satisfaction to be on the menu.

I measure my success by the positive feedback of the women who receive my message. I am excited at the thought of masses embracing their sexuality. There is strength in numbers, but the true powers lies within each individual soul that has grown bold enough to speak their truth. Despite what society and the media may have tried to sell you about being born feeble and female, women were divinely created with unparalleled power to birth nations. The force of womanhood is like no other I have witnessed in my lifetime. Look at our historical movements for change and equality for suffrage. Women are gifted with mighty big hearts to love, potent courage to protect the things we hold dear, and the fascinating fortitude to nurture those among us that go lacking. I am in awe and declare women are just magical. I have suffered loss that would have broken most and felt pain words cannot describe, but I stand today stronger and even sexier than I started.

Never be Satisfied Again

I want you to see yourself as I see you. I see the beauty and sexy in all women. Sexy is not what you wear, your hair, or scent. Sexy is your *essence*. Your smile may make you appear appealing to the human eye, but your affectionate nature is the real magnetism that attracts others who desire your touch. Your ability to express passion and desire will make others crave your presence in their space. You should not feel ashamed of such natural emotions. Humans are born with a need for human touch. When babies are born, immediate skin-to-skin time with mother has been proven to improve the wellbeing of both baby and new mom. Just as firm handshakes and steady eye contact are behaviors we associate with honesty and integrity, hot kisses and warm caresses communicate a shared fondness. If you want to really get your sexy back, learn to proficiently articulate your admiration of the human form. Beyond fondling the intimate areas of your own body and your partner, I challenge you to seduce the soul. Seduction requires the art of persuasion. Stimulate your spiritual being with constant affirmations. I have found the best way to coax anyone into compliance begins with a clearly stated request, followed by proven rewards. When that person knows exactly what you want and expect of them, as well as what they should expect to receive in return, you have optimized their likelihood to acquiesce.

So speak up, and demand your heart's desire. I demand that you know your body inside and out. Get a mirror and see your beautiful flower of a sex. Caress each petal and massage your budding clitoris. I need you open your mind to all the possibilities of what your empowered sexuality can conquer. I hope you can reconcile how your spirit being and sexual essence are two sides of the same coin. Your heart pumps both blood and passion. Without both, you are not alive. Your spirit feeds on faith while your sexuality thrives on fulfilled desire and stimulation. If you do the work and commit to bolstering your physical, mental, spiritual and sexual health, the rewards to be reaped are endless. Good health, peace of mind, and a self-assured path to success are just a few rewards of comprehensive wellness. My desire is for you to be healthy and sexually fulfilled, but I hope you never become satisfied or complacent with any station in life. I want you to have an unquenchable thirst and insatiable appetite for pleasure because I am confident your best sex and best life await you. As our time together comes to an end, know that I am here rooting for your success. Turn yet another page in your book of life and start again.

The End

ACKNOWLEDGEMENTS

I must acknowledge my parents. I will forever be a daddy's girl. My dad was and still is my hero. My dad taught me how to love a woman. He *told* me he loved me often, but he *showed* me even more. The manner in which he treated my mother showed me how a woman should be adored. I miss him every day, and I live to make him proud. My mother is my backbone. I am the physician, author, entrepreneur, and mother I am because you, Nora Hall, have loved me through both good and bad times. It has been a joy to in turn help you become a successful single hot mama. Your journey inspired this book. Your help and presence in both my own and my daughter's life allowed me to complete with homage to the strongest lady I know.

I also have to acknowledge my grandparents. Alfred Hall II, my grandfather, always told me I was something special. My maternal grandmother, Lula Mae Young, will always be the original hot girl. Fourteen children, one husband, and a couple baby-daddies never stopped her hustle or her grind. The most important lesson she lived taught me to always keep it moving.

I could never forget my brother. Andre Hall you are my right hand. You keep me grounded, while pushing me to reach for the stars.

My Ava Grace. Baby girl you prove to me each and every day anything is possible, and sometimes we have to make our own magic.

Larry, Carol and Destinee. Unbeknownst to you, this piece of literature was birthed in your basement. I thank you for the solace I have frequently found in your home that allowed my creativity to manifest on paper to be shared with the world. I thank you for providing room and board during my studies at University of Michigan. I am grateful for all of my Michigan family – my relatives, my church community, and my women's group. Your unwavering support will never be forgotten. Also, thank you for loving my baby girl like your own.

My physician council of advisors who maintain my physical and mental health: Drs. Michael Young, Omari Young, Richard Turner, Tiffany Wilson, Kelsey Webb, Erin Olivier, and Katherine Thimmesch.

My village people: Mickey, Alex, Melinda, and Donald. Thank you.

The ecstatic, orgasmic, 2014 and 2015 cohorts of Sex Therapists, Counselors and Educators at University of Michigan School of Social Work taught me more than anyone probably ever wants to know about sex. I appreciate the shared knowledge and life experiences that cumulated into the most titillating educational experience of my career. Sallie Field and Valerie Wood, thank you for never letting me give up. I am probably going to need lifelong supervision. Love you all!

The Almighty Real HU, Howard University. Your College of Medicine made a physician. Your campus birthed my spiritual quest to sexual empowerment. Know that!

I know there will be someone or two or three I left out…So, universe, I thank you!

ABOUT THE AUTHOR

Dr. KaNisha L. Hall is a native of Shreveport, Louisiana. Her earliest career as a church musician began at the age of twelve. Her music was one of many creative outlets. She has been composing and arranging since early grade school. Her scholarly activity includes a Bachelor of Science (B.S.) in Chemistry, Post-Baccalaureate Certificate, International fellowship in Cytology at Kitasato University in Japan, and Doctorate of Medicine (M.D.) from Howard University. Her family calls her a perpetual student. While maintaining her clinical practice of Anesthesiology in South Louisiana she managed to obtain a Master of Art (M.A.) in Counseling and complete focused training specifically for sexuality counseling. Her desire to promote a comprehensive clinical and sexual health to the masses has propelled her to recent notoriety.

This hardworking musician, scientist, physician, counselor, and mother multitasks her medical practice and speaking engagements. She travels around the country speaking to women about embracing their sexuality. She also tries to share her knowledge with practicing healthcare professionals to properly incorporate sexual health into their practices. Somehow she also has found time to launch hair and skin care lines, as well as begin collaborations for sexual health devices and accessories. She takes her mission to enlighten and empower women beyond words. She wants to give them the tools to fulfill their wildest dreams.

www.ingramcontent.com/pod-product-compliance
Lightning Source LLC
Chambersburg PA
CBHW050647160426
43194CB00010B/1845